*the Deeper Life*

the Deeper Life

Nancie Carmichael

TYNDALE HOUSE PUBLISHERS, INC.
WHEATON, ILLINOIS

Visit Tyndale's exciting Web site at www.tyndale.com

Edited by Lynn Vanderzalm and Sue Taylor
Designed by Jackie Noe

The meditations in this book are adapted from material previously published in *Virtue* magazine.

Library of Congress Cataloging-in-Publication Data

Carmichael, Nancie.
    The deeper life / Nancie Carmichael.
      p. cm.
    ISBN-0-8423-8586-X (sc. : alk. paper)
    1. Christian women Prayer-books and devotions—English.
 I. Title.
    BV4527.C28   1999
    242'.643—dc21   99-34603

Printed in the United States of America

05   04   03   02   01   00   99
 7   6   5   4   3   2   1

Contents ✣

Acknowledgments

I must give credit where credit is due. I owe Betsy West—first a reader of my columns and now a dear friend—thanks for her encouragement to put these thoughts from my Deeper Life columns in a book. I owe Lynn Vanderzalm, my cherished friend and editor, sincere thanks for her direction. Thank you also to Sue Taylor, for her assistance in the editing process. And most especially to my precious family, without whom there would be no columns, I owe my undying gratitude. Thank you.

Comments from Nancie's Readers

For nearly a decade, Nancie Carmichael's thoughts and insights in The Deeper Life column in *Virtue* magazine have touched the hearts of thousands of women. Listen to what some of them say about how God used her writing to comfort them, give them direction, and draw them closer to Himself:

"Reading Nancie Carmichael's articles is like getting a letter from a friend. The articles help me understand that God has a purpose in every situation in my life, even in painful interruptions." —ANNA

"I appreciate Nancie's honesty in writing about her feelings so that others can know that they are not alone. One of her articles helped me overcome a fear that was hampering me." —MARILYN

"Nancie's writings speak directly to my heart. The Scripture passages she quotes are often the very ones the Lord is speaking to me. Her sensitivity to the Spirit touches my life in a profound way." —MARY ANN

"The Deeper Life column has challenged, inspired, and encouraged me in my spiritual walk with God, in how I view my children and husband, and in who I am as a woman." —DEBRA

"I devour my Virtue magazine when it comes, with the exception of Nancie's column. I set it aside until I know I have quiet time alone so that I can savor each line. It has meant a great deal to me that Nancie is so real and shares such personal parts of her life."—JEANETTE

"I've recently been going through a very difficult time in my life and was able to refocus and recharge my relationship with Christ by rereading the past five years of my Virtue magazines, especially Nancie Carmichael's column. Her candor and spiritual wisdom were both a comfort and inspiration to me."—MARGERY

"I have kept every issue that Virtue published. Nancie Carmichael's articles have been a lifeline for me. She has been a mentor for me, helping me develop into a godly woman."—DANETTE

"I just finished reading Nancie Carmichael's article, and it brought tears to my eyes. She put into words beautifully what I have felt so often but couldn't put into words. I enjoy her articles because they challenge me, and I know the Lord is using them in my life."—BETTY

"For many years, Nancie Carmichael's writing has been a source of strength and encouragement for me. During times when I felt alone and broken-hearted, seeing her manage trials with strength and humility gave me the courage to press on. Words cannot express what it has meant to me that she has been willing to share her heart."—MARY

"One of Nancie's articles hit me in a very powerful way. It brought to me the last phase of answers and healing for the pain I have experienced in the crib death of a son many years ago. The article was an answer to prayer."—CHERYL

Be prepared to laugh, to cry, to be challenged, to be inspired, to be changed. Most of all, be prepared to have God touch you in profound ways as you read these devotionals adapted from Nancie Carmichael's writings about the deeper life.

Introduction: Growing through a Deeper Life

This book is the result of a journey that began over twenty years ago, when my husband, Bill, and I began publishing several family magazines. Of those magazines, the dearest to me was *Virtue,* primarily because I deeply identified with the Christian women who read the magazine. Many of them were like me—wives, mothers, women who were active participants in the church and community and were devoted to their homes.

When I began my work with *Virtue,* I wrote articles, edited, did interviews, brainstormed with our editorial team—in addition to being a wife to Bill and a mom to Jon, Eric, Chris, Andy, and Amy. I served on the local school board, did prison ministry, was involved in church activities, and so on. I was so busy working for God I didn't have time to know Him.

In 1990, when we redesigned *Virtue,* we took a survey of our readers in hopes of finding out what their needs were so that we could write articles to meet those needs. Among other things, we learned that our readers were feeling exhausted and stressed out and that they needed inspiration, not more things to do.

Their responses resonated within me. *I* was feeling exhausted and stressed too. I was also feeling the need to learn *from* God, not to do more things *for* Him. It was the classic Mary-Martha imbalance. I was clearly a Martha—I was busy doing good things, but inwardly I was growing more and more resentful and angry because more people weren't "helping" and I was swamped. I was discovering that when I tried to gain favor with God through what I did, there was never a finish line. I could never do enough. I could never be good enough.

I knew something very important was missing in my life, but I didn't know how to fix it. A quote from Henri Nouwen's book *Seeds of Hope* describes what was going on inside me:

> There seems to be a mountain of obstacles preventing people from being where their hearts want to be. It is so painful to watch and experience. The astonishing thing is that the battle for survival has become so "normal" that few people really believe that it can be different. . . . Oh how important is discipline,

community, prayer, silence, caring presence, simple listening, adoration, and deep, lasting faithful friendship. We all want it so much, and still the powers suggesting that all of that is fantasy are enormous. But we have to replace the battle for power with the battle to create space for the spirit.

Through a crisis with my physical health and some personal losses, I knew God was speaking to me. And I was finally ready to listen. One day when my house was quiet—unusual for our family then—I went upstairs and curled up in the big chair in the family room and wrote my first article for The Deeper Life column in *Virtue*. That article, titled "Call to Come Away," was an invitation to readers to stop their busyness, draw closer to God, and allow Him to lead them to a deeper life, a life we find as we listen to Him speaking to us in the everydayness of our lives.

The overwhelmingly positive response from our readers to that article convinced me they, too, were longing to know Jesus, not just work for Him. That article was the beginning of my writing about the deeper life.

The thirty-one meditations in this book—one

meditation for each day of a month—are adapted
from the articles I wrote for the past nine years for
The Deeper Life column in *Virtue*. The articles
flowed out of seeing the extraordinary ways God
spoke through the ordinary experiences of my life.
They express what I am learning about going deeper
with God, about listening to Him.

As I reworked these articles into a more devo-
tional format for this book, I was moved to see that
in the nine years since I wrote that first article, God
has indeed helped me to grow in ways I never
thought possible. I hope you also can see that growth
as you enter into these meditations and allow God to
draw you into a deeper life with Him. My longing is
to share with you that God can do amazing things
with us if we simply present our whole life to Him,
honestly and fully, and learn to wait on Him.

I still have a lot of growing to do. I still try to do
too much. I still lose my balance. Yet, having tasted
of the deeper life, I know I can never go back. The
more I learn of Him, the more He is showing me
what real life is—and it is often the hidden layer, the
deeper meaning that requires thought and study and
waiting to see. God does speak to us. He does so eloquently and profoundly through His Word, but also

through being still, through honest journaling and prayer, and through the common events of our lives.

My invitation to you now is the same one I issued when I wrote that first article for The Deeper Life column: Come away to a deeper life. If you'll open the eyes of your heart, God will show you how to follow Him. All you need is a heart willing to pay attention, courage to see the truth, and the choice to invite Him in—fully—to your life.

CHAPTER ONE

A Call to Come Away

*S*omething is not quite right. . . . I have a wonderful husband, five beautiful children, a satisfying job,
faithful friends, and a lovely home. My life is great!

I'm a good Christian. I try to be a good neighbor.
I bake cookies for my daughter's class. I get the
family to church (not an easy task). I teach Sunday
school and play the piano for Sunday worship.

But there is a disquieting flaw in my seemingly
perfect life. Deep inside, something seems to be
missing. I do everything right, but what's it all for?
If only I could measure my life. I remember how my
mother used to count the jeweled jars on her pantry

shelf: sixty-four quarts of pears, seventy quarts of peaches, thirty quarts of tomatoes. But how do I measure what I do?

Today is a quiet Saturday afternoon. The three youngest children are shopping with their father, and the oldest two are at college. I go upstairs to the family room and open the cedar chest in the corner. I dig out the photo albums and the keepsakes and spread them out on the floor—invitations for birthday parties, mementos of school programs, vacations, and basketball games. My whole life so far seems to be represented by things in this chest.

I look at my hands. They look as if they've worked hard to make it all happen—the endless meals, laundry, activities—just sheer effort to craft . . . what? The albums and programs next to my hands seem significant somehow.

But what does this all mean, Lord? I whisper, tears filling my eyes. *I want my life to count for something. What really lasts? What in life is really worth the effort?*

I envision Jesus sitting next to me, and I say to Him, "Jesus, something is wrong! My life is tasteless. There's no reason to feel this way. You have given me so much. And here I sit, complaining."

The Lord quietly asks, "What's in that chest?"

I smile indulgently. "Oh, family treasures." I take out the clay pot that Eric made when he was four. It's a lumpy little thing, with no earthly use other than the fact that a little boy with a shock of blond hair gave it to me—his eyes shining with love.

"What are those?" the Lord asks.

I dig out the macramé hanger Jon made in the first grade, the paper lion Amy colored, a book of poems Chris wrote, and a watercolor Andy painted.

"Oh, treasures from my children. Just little things, trinkets, really. They're not important to anyone but their father and me. And only because they're reminders."

As I think about my children, the miracle of each one—their laughter, their faith, their love—something warm and complete begins to form in my heart. I am overcome by how much I love them and how much they love me. And suddenly I realize, *That is enough.*

"Lord," I exclaim, "such wonderful children!"

The Lord laughs. "Yes. Like you!"

"Me?"

"Yes! You're wonderful!" Then a shadow crosses His face. "But you're busy." He's quiet a moment, then He says softly, "You've given Me treasures, and

I accept them, just as you accept gifts from your children." He leans forward. "But I enjoy this best: you sitting here with Me. I have so much to tell you—how to live, how to love the people around you, for My sake." His arms are open. "It's your face I want to see, your voice I long to hear. I love *you.*"

*I*N THE MIDST OF OUR BUSY LIVES,
GOD CALLS US TO COME
AWAY TO KNOW HIM MORE DEEPLY.

I put the things back into the cedar chest, quietly wondering, *Does He love me that much—as much as I love my children? Are all the things I do just trinkets in a box? Am I enough?*

I walk downstairs and go outside. The air is warm and fragrant with the musky scent of freshly fallen pine needles. Autumn is approaching and, behind it, winter. But now I sense a fresh touch, a promise.

"Jesus," I whisper, "I think I understand. I love You, too."

Take some time to examine your own life—how you are spending your time and energy. Perhaps you, too, want to find balance. Perhaps you, too, long to know that your life has significance. Perhaps you, too, long to know Jesus more deeply rather than just know *about* Him or just do things *for* Him.

Life has a way of keeping us from quality time with Jesus. We are busy, with many commitments. But we can grow deeper in our life with Him. Open your heart to Him. Listen for His voice. Rest in His presence with you.

 Lord, thank You that in Your love for us, You draw close to us and want to lead us into a deeper life with You. We want to know You more fully, Lord. Speak to us in the everyday experiences in our lives. We open our hearts and ears to hear You. Amen.

Come to me . . . and I will give you rest. . . .
Let me teach you, because I am humble and gentle,
and you will find rest for your souls.

MATTHEW 11:28-29, NLT

ALL OF US ARE WILLING TO ADMIT PANGS OF HUNGER
AND FEELINGS OF EMPTINESS INSIDE US. . . . OBVIOUSLY,
GOD DOES NOT INTEND TO SATISFY THIS DESIRE COMPLETELY
IN THIS WORLD; ITS FUNCTION IS TO DRAW US CLOSER AND
CLOSER TO GOD WHO ALONE CAN GIVE US COMPLETE
SATISFACTION. . . . SOMETIMES WE FORGET THAT GOD
COMES TO US, NOT ONLY TO GIVE US PEACE BUT ALSO
TO DISTURB US. HE COMFORTS THE AFFLICTED AND
HE AFFLICTS THE COMFORTABLE.

John Powell, *A Reason to Live! A Reason to Die!*

CHAPTER TWO

Seeking a Grateful Heart

I was born at Thanksgiving in the late forties. In those days mothers were kept in the hospital two weeks after giving birth and were not even allowed up. Maybe that's why Mother cherished the birth of each of her seven children—she probably didn't get any other vacation from the farmwork she faced every day. Mom had been a city girl before she married my father, a blue-eyed Swedish farmer, who moved her out to his spread, with no running water or indoor plumbing. Through isolated bitter winters and hot summers, she and Dad coaxed their living out of a sometimes unyielding Montana soil.

One day I drove to Mother's house to bring her to my home for the weekend. By this time she was seventy-seven, a widow, and had retired to Oregon. Under the primary care of my oldest sister, she needed all seven of us children to take turns helping to parent her. I hugged her thin body, willing energy and health to her.

"Oh!" she laughed, "I'm so glad you're here." She was always delighted to have any of her children or grandchildren near.

"Come on, Mom. I'm taking you home with me for a few days."

She still had the ready smile and laugh of a teen-ager, even though she'd struggled with chronic leukemia for years. Often she was deathly ill, only to recover with amazing resilience and return from the hospital to her little apartment with her cat, her canary, and stacks of crossword puzzles.

Now, however, Mother was unable even to fix her-self a cup of tea, and the doctor thought she might have Alzheimer's as well. Thirteen years ago Mother had sat by Dad's bed as he was taken by cancer. Lately she was talking increasingly about him. "You know . . . I remember the time. I knew—" she felt her way around the words—"Oh, I can't *think*. I know what I want to say. . . . "

The drive to my house took two hours, and I urged Mom to rest along the way. "Oh no. I don't want to miss anything. The trees . . . the sky . . . so beautiful!"

I found myself watching her delight in her surroundings as we drove past lakes and streams and up winding mountain roads. The brilliant yellows and reds of the vine maple shot out like flames against the dark green of the hillside.

"You know," Mother said, turning to me as if she'd just thought of something, "we had seven children" (she still speaks for Dad), "and they all love the Lord and have wonderful families. Isn't that great?"

"Yes, Mom." I was quietly amused, thinking, *She's told me this a thousand times. Mom, I'm not so wonderful. I'm moody. Sometimes I get weary of well doing and wonder if my children are gifts or plagues—if my husband is my sweet love or an irritant.*

As we drove, I reflected on a documentary about euthanasia I'd watched recently. The reporter told how a lady with Alzheimer's had asked her doctor to help her commit suicide. I looked at Mom. She

9

hated losing her memory. Her once keen mind that won every board game and could explain difficult passages from Revelation now struggled to name each of her children.

Lord, I silently queried, *what goes here? Following You is supposed to be a joyous, satisfying life. From glory to glory, You said, as we behold Your face. Is it getting better, God, for Mom? Or are we now on a slow slide of deterioration?*

WHEN OUR EYES AND HEARTS ARE OPEN
TO SEE GOD'S BLESSINGS,
WE WILL BE AMAZED AT HIS GOODNESS TO US.

A few days later I found a suitcase full of old letters Mom had sent me over the years. She was a good writer, honest with her emotions. She worried. She steamed. She struggled with self-doubt and self-esteem. She was full of ambitious longing. But woven through it all, I could see her sense of humor and her underlying rock-solid certainty that Jesus Christ, her anchor, was the giver of all good things.

My mother was a charming person, and I think the fact that she was filled with gratitude made her that way. In that weekend at our house, I was amazed to see that now, of all the times in her life when she could have been bitter or angry, Mother was instead overwhelmingly grateful. Grateful for her family. Grateful for God's beautiful world. Grateful for the canned soup I heated for her lunch. ("Oh, this is wonderful, Nancie!") I felt guilty; it seemed such a small thing.

I gulped down my soup and rushed on to my "to do" list, impatiently curtailing my activities and responsibilities to fit Mother's slower pace as she focused on a flower, the sunshine, my daughter's face cupped in her hands. My mother taught me many things, and now, in what had to be one of the most difficult phases of her life, she showed me that it's possible to have a heart of gratitude toward God in all circumstances.

Perhaps you are like me, and you find it hard at times to be grateful. Gratitude gets lost when we refuse to see the beauty and goodness in everyday life—even in the difficult times. Sometimes it takes discipline and a conscious effort to be grateful. Maybe we don't really see what we have until we see what we have lost. But once you open your heart to see the blessings God gives, you will be amazed— charmed—by how

rich and full your life is. I pray that your life will be
rich with gratitude . . . for God is indeed *good.*

> Lord, it is Your will that we praise
> You, continually and in all things. Help
> us not to wait for the "right moment" or
> withhold the praise that You so deserve.
> You are a good God, and You give us all
> things—from the very air we breathe to
> the food that we eat. May we cultivate
> a spirit of gratitude toward You always:
> in difficult times, in good times, in times
> of joy and times of frustration. Lord,
> open our eyes to see the blessings You
> give, that we may praise You for Your
> goodness to us. Amen.

Let us continually offer the sacrifice of praise to God, that is,
the fruit of our lips, giving thanks to His name.

HEBREWS 13:15

TO BE GRATEFUL IS TO RECOGNIZE THE LOVE OF GOD IN
EVERYTHING HE HAS GIVEN US—AND HE HAS GIVEN US
EVERYTHING. EVERY BREATH WE DRAW IS A GIFT OF HIS LOVE,
EVERY MOMENT OF EXISTENCE IS A GIFT OF GRACE, FOR IT
BRINGS WITH IT IMMENSE GRACES FROM HIM. GRATITUDE
THEREFORE TAKES NOTHING FOR GRANTED, IS NEVER
UNRESPONSIVE, IS CONSTANTLY AWAKENING TO NEW WONDER
AND TO PRAISE OF THE GOODNESS OF GOD.

Thomas Merton, *Thoughts in Solitude*

CHAPTER THREE

The Everlasting Arms of Grace

*B*ill and I were leaving for a weekend speaking engagement. The final preparations were almost completed when Amy, then six years old, began acting up. She jumped up and down on the bed, deliberately messing things I had laid out for the trip. I sternly corrected her, then went to the kitchen to serve dinner. Amy followed me, her little face a storm cloud as she grabbed her place setting off the table and put it back on the counter. I was about to lose my patience when I realized something was troubling her deeply.

I got down on the floor where she was sitting, took

her in my arms, and looked into her dark eyes. "Amy," I said softly, "what is wrong?"

She threw her arms around me and burst into sobs. "Don't leave me, Mommy! Please don't leave me!"

My heart broke for her. I understood how vulnerable she felt at the idea of being "left." She had been abandoned as a baby and had spent the first three years of her life in a Korean orphanage. My love seemed so inadequate to fill the deep emotional hole that an abandoned child is left with. I felt helpless, not knowing what to offer except my assurances *again*. How could I convince her, how could I make her *know* I would never abandon her, that I would come back?

Suddenly Amy stopped sniffling and looked up at me, surprised. "Hey—why are *you* crying?"

"Amy, I feel sad because you are sad. But I promise you I will never stop being your mother, and I love you, always."

"Oh, Mommy, I love you, too!" She kissed me exuberantly, jumped up, and ran off to play, all smiles. And there I sat, on the floor, wondering what her sudden change was all about!

I think I know. When Amy was honest with me

about her fears, my tears and my loving arms showed her that I identified with what she was feeling. They also showed that I loved and accepted her just as she is. Her expression of vulnerability and need did not make me love her any less. When she realized that someone understood how she felt, she experienced immense relief. That was a healing moment in her life because it was another step on the path toward a growing assurance that she was wanted and loved.

We all long to be understood, to know that some-one cares how we feel. The experience with Amy reminded me that our beautiful High Priest, Jesus, literally "got down" where we lived, became human, and therefore understands our feelings. His nail-scarred hands prove His love for us. He longs for us to know that He cares, that we can run to Him in our weakness and humanness, and that He will always be there, loving and accepting us.

It is His plan, His design, that we accept His love and, in turn, offer it to others. But how do we do that? Jesus knows the truth about us, and still He loves and accepts us when we truly come to Him. If we are to be understood by others, we must risk facing—and telling—the truth about ourselves.

*THE UNCONDITIONAL LOVE OF OUR GREAT
HIGH PRIEST, DEMONSTRATED BY HIS
NAIL-SCARRED HANDS, ENABLES US TO
EXPRESS THAT LOVE TO OTHERS AND
RECEIVE IT FROM THEM.*

Some time ago two friends and I were having tea and discussing what the body of Christ really meant—how we need to be honest with each other and really listen to and care for one another. One of my friends said, "I feel for you, Nancie, because some people put you on a pedestal. That must be hard."

That was my opening to tell my "real" truth. I took a deep breath. "Well, frankly, I'm not doing very well. My pride keeps insisting, 'I can handle this difficulty; I can solve that problem,' but I can't." Then I broke down and cried. My friends put their arms around me and prayed for me. Their arms, their prayers said it all. When they left to go home, my burden was lighter. My laughter was real and my smile genuine. What a wonderful thing is it to be loved, warts and all.

Amy received healing because she was able to articulate her deep fears to someone who cared. I received healing as I confessed to my friends that I didn't have it all together. James 5:16 says: "Confess your faults to one another, and pray for one another, that you may be healed" (KJV).

Our transient, busy lives make it difficult to find safe places to confess our needs. We struggle with some common misconceptions: "If I'm honest about the way I really feel, she won't want to be friends with me." Or "I was vulnerable once, and she betrayed my confidence, so never again." And it can be costly to truly listen to another's pain because often there isn't an easy solution. Real listening can make you feel helpless.

Out of that experience with Amy and, later, having tea with my friends, I learned that to experience true healing, I must tell the truth. I also realized that I can be part of others' healing by having the courage to respond to the honest feelings they express. Once I have done that, I can more fervently pray for them.

What about you? Do you know God's unconditional love and grace? Have you felt God's arms around you through the loving acceptance another person has shown you? Now think about someone who may need *you* to be God's arms of understanding and love. Is it one of your children? Is it your husband?

Is it a coworker or neighbor or friend? Ask God to allow you to be the extension of His everlasting arms to someone today.

Lord, I know You want us to know Your unconditional love . . . to experience it deep in our hearts. Help us to truly receive Your grace by allowing You into those places where we are most weak and vulnerable, where we most need Your cleansing and healing.

Give us the courage to be open with others—to receive Your love and grace from them as we see and speak the truth about ourselves. And then, Lord, help us to offer healing and grace to others by offering them our presence and our prayers. In Christ's name, amen.

We do not have a high priest who is unable to sympathize with our weaknesses, but we have one who has been tempted in every way, just as we are—yet was without sin. Let us then approach the throne of grace with confidence, so that we may receive mercy and find grace to help us in our time of need.

HEBREWS 4:15-16, NIV

IN AGAPE LOVE THERE CAN BE NO PRIDE. FOR BY ITS VERY NATURE IT PRODUCES HUMILITY. . . . WE TAKE IT AS RECIPIENTS OF GRACE. WE BECOME LITTLE CHILDREN AND . . . EMPTY OUR HANDS OF ALL OUR STRIVING, ALL OUR GOODNESS, ALL OUR WORKS—WE RECEIVE THE GIFT OF GOD. AND WHEN THAT GRACE OF GOD ENTERS OUR HEARTS IT IS SO UNMERITED, SO OVERWHELMINGLY GRACIOUS, THAT IT SENDS US TO OUR KNEES IN DEEPEST GRATITUDE.

E. Stanley Jones, *Christian Maturity*

CHAPTER FOUR

Open Hands, Trusting Heart

I remember first being slam-dunked by fear when my husband, Bill, went to Africa for a month-long missions trip. I was eight months pregnant, so I stayed home with our two young sons. I'd awaken suddenly at night, sure there was an intruder in the house. The fear was choking, paralyzing. In the morning I would chide myself, "Silly. You're a grown woman."

It's one thing to reason with fear in the daytime; it is quite another to do so when it strikes you unexpectedly and logic has no effect whatsoever on it.

I cannot recall being afraid as a child or a

teenager, other than experiencing the normal stresses related to piano recitals and geometry. Real dangers seemed as remote as the moon. But here I was, many years later, developing a worried brow. I was a strong believer in Jesus Christ, but little things chipped away at my peace of mind. I began to realize that the world could be an ugly place. And as a mother, I was determined to protect my own from the world: "What should I do about Chris's chronic ear infections?" "Will Eric outgrow this allergy?" "Am I handling their discipline right?"

One of the problems with anxiety is that it feeds itself. Legitimate concern can turn into worry. Worry becomes anxiety. And anxiety is a fiery dart the enemy can use to dominate our life. It often comes disguised as "caring" about some issue we are dealing with, but over time my fears grew so that my life became paralyzed. I was terrified to drive on freeways, and there were times I wondered how I could cope.

My friend Clare noticed the dark circles under my eyes and asked what was wrong.

"I can't sleep," I confessed. "I wake up terrified."

Clare reached for her Bible with a determined look. "Fear is not of God," she said. "I know. I used to struggle with it. Here's a Scripture passage that helped me," and she read 2 Timothy 1:7: "'For God has not given us a spirit of fear, but of power and of love and of a sound mind.' Memorize this verse, and if you wake up afraid, just tell Satan to get lost. He'll leave you alone."

Amazingly, it worked, and I slept untroubled. I began to memorize other Scripture verses that addressed my fears, posting them on my refrigerator and on the dashboard of my car. God's Word became a powerful force that kept fear from destroying my life. And little by little, my fears began to evaporate.

FEAR CAN KEEP YOU FROM ALL THAT
GOD INTENDS FOR YOU.

I've found that life never stops presenting opportunities to fear. I don't like to fly, but I have to do it a lot. Speaking in front of hundreds of people scares me, but I continue to do it because I feel it's what God wants me to do. And yet in each area of fear—each area of growth—I am presented with an opportunity to let go and trust God. And He is always there. Even though some of my children are young adults, I still find myself worrying about them. Parenting is fertile soil for fear. But it's also a great opportunity to do the hardest, truest, and best loving—loving with trust—and cast my cares on Jesus. I have to keep coming back to these core questions: *Who's really in charge? Is God indeed the Lord of all?*

Fear can keep you from being and doing all that God intends for you. Do certain fears grip your life? When you lie alone at night, what fears come to your mind? Try this: Look up specific Scripture verses that speak about those fears. Make a point of memorizing them, and meditate on the provision that your heavenly Father offers you: His deliverance . . . His salvation . . . His protection.

Fear can also offer a powerful opportunity to realize that we need to grow in a certain area. We have a choice—we can allow fear to keep us boxed in, or we can confront it in the strength of God's Word and the power of His name. Instead of a place of defeat, it can be a place of growth and spiritual development. Dare to trust God to calm your fears, and watch your life grow. If He can help me, I know He can help you!

Father God, thank You for reminding us that You intend for us to live not in fear but in Your love. In our anxious moments, help us to remember that You are in control. Cause us to see our fears as opportunities to trust You and grow in our dependence on You. As we hide Your powerful Word in our hearts, may we find peace from our fears, and comfort in Your abiding presence with us. In Christ's name, amen.

In the multitude of my anxieties within me,
Your comforts delight my soul.

PSALM 94:19

THE NEXT HOUR, THE NEXT MOMENT, IS AS MUCH BEYOND OUR GRASP AND AS MUCH IN GOD'S CARE AS THAT A HUNDRED YEARS AWAY. CARE FOR THE NEXT MINUTE IS JUST AS FOOLISH AS CARE FOR THE MORROW, OR FOR A DAY IN THE NEXT THOUSAND YEARS—IN NEITHER CAN WE DO ANYTHING, IN BOTH GOD IS DOING EVERYTHING.

An Anthology of George Macdonald

CHAPTER FIVE

Living Life's Parentheses

*I*t was Sunday, and we were on our way home from church. I was looking forward to leisure time reading the Sunday paper and then painting the railing in the family room. We were doing a major remodeling of our home, and it seemed as if it would never end. If we could do just one thing a day, I reasoned, it would help. Today I was going to tackle that railing.

Chris broke into my thoughts. "Mom, see those bluffs over there? I've heard that's a great hike. Let's pack our lunch and go up there."

"Well, I was going to paint, but . . ." The eager look on his face weakened my resolve. "All right."

It was a late spring afternoon, the sun warm and the air sweet with the scent of wildflowers. We hurriedly changed clothes, packed our backpacks with sandwiches, drinks, the Sunday paper, and a book on Hemingway (Chris had a paper due the next day), and drove off toward the bluffs. Chris parked the car on the side of an obscure dirt road, and we set off on a trail through the manzanita bushes and ponderosa pines, wending our way up the bluff.

"Chris! Do you know where you're going?"

He was way ahead of me on the trail, his slender form stooped with his backpack, blond hair glinting in the sunlight. The trail grew steeper, and the hike turned into a climb. Before long we reached the top, breathless yet exhilarated.

"There!" Chris turned to me triumphantly. "I *thought* this was what we'd see!"

I caught my breath. Stretched far below was a vast green meadow with a river winding through it. Glistening snowcapped peaks towered above, where hawks and eagles soared on the wind. How often had I driven past these bluffs, never dreaming this was behind them?

"Chris . . ." He was busy spreading out towels on the warm rocks and arranging our lunch so we would have the best view.

"Yeah, Mom?" he inquired.

How often had I looked at him—my third son—and not seen all the wonder and beauty? How do you tell your seventeen-year-old how much you love him? How do you say, with heart-stopping realization, *My child, you are almost an adult and . . . you're wonderful!* Instead I said, "Thanks, honey, for bringing me up here."

We ate our lunch in the sun, and Chris and I talked about the future, his interests, his world. That sunny Sunday afternoon was unexpected, unplanned. But the memory of talking with my son, high on a rocky bluff, is one I will always cherish.

My mind flashed back three years to when our magazine staff was rapidly expanding. Those were exciting, exhausting days: designing layout, exploring demographics, interviewing and hiring new staff. One day an elderly woman with a cane came in the door.

"I would like to see your offices and then talk to someone about the magazines," she announced.

31

Everyone else seemed busy, so I reluctantly gave her a tour.

When we finished, I took her to my office, and she sat heavily in the chair.

> ## *O*FTEN THE "REAL EVENT" IS WHAT'S NOT ON THE CALENDAR.

"Can't walk like I used to. I had a friend drive me here," she explained. "While I was praying the other day, the Lord laid these magazines on my mind. Is it all right if I pray for them?"

Was it *all right?* We joined hands, and Flora prayed for my husband, the editors, the assistants and artists; those in Circulation, and Advertising; the writers and the readers. Flora's simple prayer brought all of us immeasurable encouragement at just the right time. What I first perceived as an interruption was really a desperately needed affirmation that God's hand was on what we were doing.

It's mysterious the way God moves in our lives. Often the "real event" is not on the calendar. It just happens—like a happening within a happening. These are life's "parentheses" that become the real agenda.

Have there been "parentheses" in your life—
unplanned, unexpected occurrences? Mark
5:24-34 tells of the chronically ill woman who
pressed through the crowd to touch Jesus. She said,
"If only I may touch His clothes, I shall be made
well." This woman was an interruption to Jesus. He
was on His way to minister to someone else, and
this woman was not a scheduled stop on the way.
Yet what happened when He responded to the
interruption became an important faith-inspiring
story recorded for us in Scripture.

Prayerfully consider what you can learn from the
way Jesus lived. He spent his earthly life responding
to interruptions and people's needs. Ask Jesus to
open your eyes to interruptions that may really be
divine appointments. And maybe, as I did that day
on the high bluff with Chris, and the day that Flora
came to visit our magazine office, you can hear God
speaking to you there.

Thank You, Lord, for intruding in our lives to show us what is truly important. Sometimes we're so focused on our own agenda that we fail to see You in the unexpected and uninvited interruptions in our lives. Father, we ask You to speak to us, however You will. We only pray that we will have the grace and wisdom to see You and hear You in the "parentheses" of life and that we will come away gladly to learn of You in those times. Amen.

I want you to know, dear brothers and sisters, that everything that
has happened to me here has helped to spread the Good News.
For everyone here, including all the soldiers in the palace guard,
knows that I am in chains because of Christ. And because of my
imprisonment, many of the Christians here have gained confidence
and become more bold in telling others about Christ.

PHILIPPIANS 1:12-14, NLT

THE GREAT THING, IF ONE CAN, IS TO STOP REGARDING ALL
THE UNPLEASANT THINGS AS INTERRUPTIONS OF ONE'S "OWN,"
OR "REAL" LIFE. THE TRUTH IS OF COURSE THAT WHAT
ONE CALLS THE INTERRUPTIONS ARE PRECISELY ONE'S REAL
LIFE—THE LIFE GOD IS SENDING ONE DAY BY DAY:
WHAT ONE CALLS ONE'S "REAL LIFE" IS A PHANTOM
OF ONE'S OWN IMAGINATION.

C. S. Lewis, *The Letters of C. S. Lewis to Arthur Greeves*

CHAPTER SIX

Dismantling My Tents

$\mathcal{O}$n my walk today I went past the old fort behind our house where our children once played. I remembered how they would come home, smelling outdoorsy and fresh from the sun and wind. Today, someone else's boys were there—hats askew, tennis shoes scruffy. I walked on, misty-eyed.

I vividly remember the day Chris started first grade. I was driving the boys to the school, baby Andy in a car seat next to me. Chris was sandwiched in the back between his two older brothers, his Bionic Man lunch pail on his lap and his eyes sparkling.

"I can't *wait* to go to school so I can learn more about Jesus," he said. My heart sank.

"You won't learn more about Jesus at this school," Jon said soberly, with older-brother authority. Eric had told him, "You're gonna hear lots of bad words, too. Just ignore them. Don't let them stay in your head."

Now, back from my walk, I had to face facts: Three of our five children have changed into . . . *men.* They shave, go to work, love to eat, and talk of college majors, transmissions going out, golf scores. They have theological discussions and ask daring questions.

These boys-turned-men rummage in the garage looking for apartment furnishings, while Bill and I console each other with thoughts of a clean house in the fall. But that season will again see our third son's leap into the world as he leaves for college a thousand miles away.

Sometimes when I want things to change, they don't. At other times change comes unbidden. . . .

The skylight in my bathroom mercilessly exposes the crinkles around my eyes. I'm doing things that are "good for me" now, somewhat the way a car buff takes care of his '56 Chevy when he knows he can no longer get replacement parts. I can see that I am changing physically. The question is, Am I growing, or am I just getting older?

I'm drawn in Scripture to the life of Abraham. It was a never-ending pilgrimage, a life characterized by moving to God-knows-where. Each time God told Abraham to move, Abraham dismantled his tents, set up housekeeping somewhere else, dug dirt out of old wells that were clogged and abandoned, and settled in until God moved him again, always closer to the land God had promised to give him. God did not allow Abraham to stay in one place; He led him through change, through testing, through conflict, through loss.

I see that happening in myself: Growth happens best in times of challenge, of difficulty. When I'm comfortable, my approach to the eternal becomes trite. Then God dismantles my "tent" of comfort, often over my protests, and says, "Move on. Grow."

Often growth is so slow that it's imperceptible to us. Sometimes, looking back, I see that I drifted from the path. Did I grow in the wrong direction? Some bitterness here, hardness of heart there, a little cynicism, a tinge of apathy?

Going back over the same ground—getting back

on the right path—and digging dirt out of wells takes work and risk: It takes courage to realize that I may have been operating under some faulty assumptions and that I need to change if living water is to flow again. The losses of life force me to reexamine my path, to redirect my growth to new possibilities in God, to daring faith in the Almighty One.

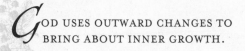

GOD USES OUTWARD CHANGES TO BRING ABOUT INNER GROWTH.

I would love to always have my children gathered around, to have them come to me for advice and comfort, to have the chairs full at the dinner table (at least on Sundays). But this is changing too. I see a faraway look in the eyes of my young men as they dare to dream big dreams for God. So I must pray, "Lord, let them always say yes to You and to the changes You will bring into their lives. For that is how they will grow."

Some of us resist change more than others, but change is a reality of life, and it gives us opportunities to grow. Think back over the last ten years of your

life, and note some of the significant changes.
Perhaps they involved growing children, job changes,
or moving to a different place and "starting over."
Change confronts us with the bottom line: What is my
source, my reason for living? And where do I go from
here? How can I grow through this challenge? Think
about how you have responded to those changes God
has brought into your life. Have you dug in your heels
and refused to see God's hand in them? Or have you,
like Abraham, "dismantled your tents" and moved
on, trusting in God's provision for you in the next
season of growth? Ask God to use what He has taught
you through outward changes to make you more
sensitive to ways you can pray for and encourage
others facing the challenge of change.

 *Lord, change often means loss
that causes us pain. Give us eyes to see
what You can do through the painful
changes in our lives. May we see
change as Your reminder to dig deeper,
to find greater intimacy with You and
strength for the next part of our journey.
In Christ's name, amen.*

One thing I do, forgetting those things which are behind and reaching forward to those things which are ahead, I press toward the goal for the prize of the upward call of God in Christ Jesus.

PHILIPPIANS 3:13–14

THE PROCESS OF GROWING UP IS TO BE VALUED FOR
WHAT WE GAIN, NOT FOR WHAT WE LOSE.

C. S. Lewis, *An Experiment in Criticism*

CHAPTER SEVEN

Singing in the Dark

It was after midnight, and our fifteen-year-old son, Andy, still wasn't home. He was out with a buddy, Isaac (who was going to spend the night), and a friend who'd just received his driver's license.

Allowing Andy to ride with a friend who drove was a new experience for us. Until now, his older brothers had always provided transportation. Andy, with his infectious grin and unquenchable enthusiasm for life, suddenly seemed much too young to be loose on the highway.

Bill and I stared at the clock by the bed and tried to remain rational. But we live more than thirty miles from the school, on isolated mountain roads! Where could they be? They were already an hour late.

"Are you awake?" Bill asked.

"Yes. Do you know the name of the boy who's driving them home?"

"No," Bill replied. "I don't even know who to call."

Visions of car wrecks filled my mind. It felt strange—helpless—to be relying on someone other than a responsible older brother for Andy's rides to and from football games. We stared again at the digital clock: 12:30. I lay there tensely, trying to ignore the knot in my stomach.

Then we heard it, way off in the distance. "What is that?" I asked. "It's not a car—"

"It sounds like . . . singing?"

Our two dogs began to bay in response.

We heard the back door open softly, then boys' muffled laughter. Andy poked his head into our bedroom. "Hey, Mom and Dad. How come you're not asleep?"

We sat up.

"Where've you been?" Bill asked. "We've been worried sick!"

44

"Oh, I'm sorry. The gate across the road was locked, and we didn't have a key, so my friend dropped us off. Isaac and I walked home—almost three miles. It was so dark we could hardly see anything except stars, but is was *awesome!* We sang all the way home."

The boys went upstairs, and Bill and I had to laugh. They were out celebrating their youth, singing under God's beautiful stars, while Bill and I, the mature ones, huddled under the blankets worrying.

What is it about the experience of singing that goes beyond words—especially a cappella singing? No props, no background instruments, just intimate communication of our thoughts to God. When we sing a hymn or praise chorus in church, we experience more than just the notes and harmonies. We join in fellowship with others in our faith walk, our adventure with God.

When we sing, "Marvelous grace of our loving Lord, grace that exceeds our sin and our guilt," I remember Grandmother Olson, an early widow who lost three children and went through the Great Depression. That song was the theme of her life.

"Great Is Thy Faithfulness" makes me think of my father, a man of the soil. I see him in the sunlight that streamed through the church window, straining with all his might for the high notes. He seemed to understand that his very life (and that of his family) depended on the seasons, upon God. And God was faithful. Always.

Sometimes the world is "too present," my heart is heavy, and I can find no words to express my feelings. Even prayer is difficult. I find my way to the piano and begin to sing: "I just want to be where You are, dwelling in Your Presence." And then we connect, God and I.

*S*ONGS OF PRAISE FROM THE DARKEST NIGHT REACH THE HEART OF GOD.

Why is it hard to sing in times of darkness? I know it is especially necessary then. I remember the cold January when Andy was a baby. My father's cancer, which we had thought was in remission, was back and unrelenting. My brothers and sisters and I took turns being with our father and watched the light in his wonderful Swedish blue eyes slowly extinguish. How he loved us, and how painful was the parting. Sitting next to my father, holding his hand, I quietly sang, "Unto Thee, O Lord, do I lift up my soul; O my God, I trust in You." Those songs—our sacrifices of praise even when we can't see the light—shoot straight up, through the darkness, to the heart of God.

What is a "dark" time for you? It's not the same for everyone. Maybe you've suffered from depression, or you've experienced a painful loss, and you can't see how any good can come from it. Perhaps you feel that God is distant—far away from where you are right now. Can you find a time to be alone with God and sing to Him? You don't need to sing happy songs. Sing from your heart. If you need help, find a hymnal and choose a song that reflects what you are feeling. Sing those words to Jesus. Sing to Him anywhere: taking a walk, driving in the car, working around the house. Scripture says that God inhabits the praises of His people, and when we praise Him in the midst of our pain, He will be there.

Lord, how often in our darkest places—our places of loneliness, confusion, and pain—You speak to our hearts most eloquently. Your presence comes and reminds us of the morning, when Your mercies are always new again. Keep us from waiting until we see what You are doing to give You praise. Give us songs of praise in the midst of our pain. Open our hearts and lives to You so that, like Paul and Silas in the darkness of their prison cell, we can sing to You even in the darkest night. In Jesus' name, amen.

I will sing to the Lord as long as I live;
I will sing praise to my God while I have my being.
May my meditation be sweet to Him;
I will be glad in the Lord.

PSALM 104:33-34

YOU TAKE THE PEN AND THE LINES DANCE.

YOU TAKE THE FLUTE, AND THE NOTES SHIMMER.

YOU TAKE THE BRUSH, AND THE COLORS SING.

SO THAT ALL THINGS HAVE MEANING AND BEAUTY IN

THAT SPACE BEYOND TIME WHERE YOU ARE.

HOW, THEN, CAN I HOLD BACK ANYTHING FROM YOU?

Dag Hammarskjöld, "God, the Artist"

CHAPTER EIGHT

The Place Where God Speaks

*I*t was a big game, but neither Bill nor I could make the six-hour drive to be there. Andy was playing junior varsity basketball and sometimes the last minute of the varsity game. That potential one minute of play was important—and we were missing it. The local radio station carried the game live, and we'd tuned in at home, even though the reception was terrible. Other frequencies kept breaking in, interfering, and we could barely make sense of the play-by-play.

At halftime Bill and I looked at each other, grabbed the car keys, and said to Amy, our

51

eleven-year-old daughter, "Let's go!" As we drove the thirty minutes toward Redmond, where the radio station was located, the reception became clearer. Finally we could hear the game in all its glory.

We pulled off the highway onto a frontage road and parked among the juniper and sagebrush that populate the high desert. Leaning back, we listened for The Big Moment. Would Andy get in? Would he score? Amy thought the whole pursuit unworthy of a Saturday evening, but we waited patiently anyway.

With less than a minute to go, the announcer said, "And now number three for the Panthers, Andy Carmichael, checks into the game." Within that minute, Andy made a three-point basket! We hugged each other, jubilant. It was worth it! We heard it! We shared the moment and then headed home, satisfied. As we drove, I thought about the act of listening: How easy it is to listen—but how difficult to hear—and going to the desert helped us hear.

The example of Bill, Amy, and me driving to the high desert to hear Andy's game reminded me of the story of Elijah in 1 Kings 19. Elijah was running to the wilderness to escape from wicked Queen Jezebel and finally stopped to rest under a juniper—a dry, prickly desert tree with a gnarled trunk and needles that drop everywhere. There Elijah prayed that he might die. Instead, an angel brought him food and water, nourishment from the Lord. Then Elijah continued on his journey to the mountains.

I long to hear from God. But where do I hear Him most clearly—without interference? When things are going well, I don't listen so intently. Scripture says God was not in the great wind, the earthquake, or the fire. It was afterward, when God spoke to him in a still, small voice, that Elijah received further orders and was prepared to respond.

Like Elijah, I hear God most clearly when I'm in a desert place—in pain or at the end of myself, wondering what on earth I'm doing there and knowing only that I desperately need to hear from God.

As W. H. Auden writes: "It is where we are wounded that God speaks to us."

I don't like the desert places. But that is where we are left without life's distractions, the clamoring interferences. How often I rush out of the desert toward the mountains without waiting to be nourished by Him, when all the while the desert is precisely the place where God wants to feed us for the journey.

*S*OMETIMES WE HEAR GOD MOST CLEARLY IN THE DESERT.

Don't resist the struggles or the desert places in your life. They are a gift to you, an opportunity to grow more deeply in your relationship with God. Do you find yourself in a desert place? If so, have you asked God what He may be saying to you there? If we truly want to hear from God, we must also be willing to respond to what He says to us, to see time spent in the desert as God's way of preparing us for the next leg of the journey.

Listening to God means being patient in the desert experience. Find time to be still and wait on Him; look for ways in which God is nourishing you in that dry place, and you will come to know Him more intimately as you clearly hear His voice.

Lord, we say we want to hear from You, but how we resist the desert! And yet that is where we finally can focus on what You are saying through the hard places of our lives. May we have the courage and patience to wait on You—to use time spent in the desert to dig into Your Word and allow Your truth into the most wounded, painful places of our lives. And then, in obedience to what You have spoken to our hearts, may we respond, growing into more fruitful and effective people of God. In Christ's name, amen.

We must give the more earnest heed
to the things we have heard.

HEBREWS 2:1

HE IS THE SOURCE OF ALL PEACE.

WHERE IS THIS PEACE TO BE FOUND?

IN OUR OWN WEAKNESS,

IN THOSE PLACES WHERE WE FEEL MOST BROKEN,

MOST INSECURE, MOST IN AGONY, MOST AFRAID.

Henri J. M. Nouwen, *Seeds of Hope*

CHAPTER NINE

Leaving Home, Going Home

I kiss my daughter, still snuggled in her bed, her hair a dark, tousled mass, and look in on Andy, deep in the wholehearted sleep of a growing teenager. I walk downstairs, where two of our older sons are leaving for work, and I stretch tall to hug them good-bye.

Bill drives me to the airport in the early dawn, and we share a fragrant cup of coffee and conversation as we drive. We have anxieties about parenting growing-up children. We haven't done this before, and it's scary. How do we let go? I feel a twinge of guilt—this seems like a bad time to leave the family.

But this weekend is a reunion of the little country school I attended for eight years, and I don't want to miss it. Besides, I really want to go back home to the farm. It's been a long time.

I watch people in the airport—families tearing apart, coming together, separating, reuniting. A woman cries as she says good-bye to a man. A group of college boys, their faces fresh and optimistic, hurry by with backpacks slung over their shoulders. A young couple with two small children lug diaper bags, a stroller, and toys. I recall the days when our children were small and feel a sudden longing for those days.

My mother and sister arrive on their connecting flight, and I guide my aging mother through the security gate as I would a small child, encouraging, coaxing.

She can't understand the wait. "When are we there?"

"Soon, Mother."

"I want to go home."

Home? Where is home?

My brother Dan meets us at the airport in this ruggedly magnificent place that nurtured us. I drink in the view—the rolling plains, the majestic Rockies to the west, the farm where I grew up—Dan and his wife, Nancy, have tended it well.

Early the next morning, I make my way down the familiar graveled road, past the farmhouse. The air is full of the meadowlark's song as I walk over to where the little country school used to be. It has been moved off its foundation and is now a Baptist church in a neighboring town. All that remains is a gaping, open basement. Memories flood me. I look into that impossibly small hole and remember having my feelings and knuckles bruised in a box hockey game one snowy winter afternoon . . . *right there* . . . over by that wall. Here we memorized Tennyson, Sandburg, Whitman. We laughed, played, and formed a strong sense of community.

I remember walking along this very road after I graduated from high school. I looked at the landmarks of home, the wheat fields broken by clumps of trees that marked our neighbors' places, and thought, *I love home, but I'm going to leave it.* And I did.

The reunion was marked by laughter and amazement that all of us were now middle aged. As the time came for me to fly back to Oregon, I realized I was homesick; I missed Bill, the children, my own comfortable, familiar home.

As I flew over the snowcapped Three Sisters Mountains toward home, I thought of my childhood dream—to have a "house dedicated to God," a sheltered, safe place for my family to grow. I wanted it to be a place of learning, of laughter, of music. On my walks I deliberately took a route that brought me home through the trees behind our house, where I would stop and pray: *Bless this house, Lord. May our home be a place where Your love reigns.*

WE ALL LONG FOR THE SECURITY OF HOME—BUT WHERE IS HOME?

Lately, I feel as if this place I'm praying for has become a depot instead of a home. Suitcases and duffel bags are always at the ready as people come and go. My growing children are leaving home. It's natural; it's time, but it is painful. I struggle with the transitions—the connecting flights that take me—where? And often I beg, "Let me go back, Lord, to that familiar place—the way it used to be."

But I am seeing that this "house dedicated to God" that I have so wanted to craft . . . is *me*. And unless the Lord builds the house, those who build it labor in vain. So Jesus is gently shaping me, cleansing me, and helping me to understand that in the shifting sands of time, through all the transitions, He alone is my eternal home.

What do you consider your true home? In your desire for security, are you tempted to hold tightly to the past, to what is familiar? If our hands are going to be free to grab on to what God has next for us, we need to let go of those things. These "in-between" places are powerful reminders that He is our security, our true home forever.

 Lord, we remember that You left Your heavenly home to come to earth, and in Your years of public ministry, You had no place to lay Your head—You simply did the will of the Father. We thank You for our earthly homes, our families. Help us, Lord, to hold loosely to the good things that You place in our hands—our children, our families, the places in which we live. Remind us that You are our true, everlasting home. May we keep our eyes on You and seek to do Your will. In Jesus' name, amen.

Lord, You have been our dwelling place in all generations.

PSALM 90:1

DEAR LORD, I WILL REMAIN RESTLESS,
TENSE AND DISSATISIFED UNTIL I CAN BE TOTALLY
AT PEACE IN YOUR HOUSE. BUT I AM STILL ON THE ROAD, STILL
JOURNEYING, TIRED AND WEARY AND STILL WONDERING IF I WILL
EVER MAKE IT TO THE CITY ON THE HILL. WITH VINCENT VAN
GOGH, I KEEP ASKING YOUR ANGEL, WHOM I MEET ON THE ROAD,
"DOES THE ROAD GO UPHILL THEN ALL THE WAY?" AND THE
ANSWER IS: "YES, TO THE VERY END." AND I ASK AGAIN, "AND WILL
THE JOURNEY TAKE ALL DAY LONG?" AND THE ANSWER IS: "FROM
MORNING TILL NIGHT, MY FRIEND." THERE IS NO CERTAINTY THAT
MY LIFE WILL BE ANY EASIER IN THE YEARS AHEAD, OR THAT MY
HEART WILL BE ANY CALMER. BUT THERE IS THE CERTAINTY THAT
YOU ARE WAITING FOR ME AND WILL WELCOME ME HOME WHEN
I HAVE PERSEVERED IN MY LONG JOURNEY TO YOUR HOUSE. AMEN.

Henry J. M. Nouwen, *A Cry for Mercy*

CHAPTER TEN

On the Ragged Edge

*L*ast Sunday afternoon when I went for a walk, there was a chill in the air, an unexpected smattering of snowflakes after an afternoon of sunshine. Seasons in the mountains are unpredictable—springlike one minute, wintery the next. As I walked toward home, I stopped on the edge of a clearing in a grove of trees. There on the grass in front of the house were our two youngest children, Amy, twelve, and Andy, sixteen, and our two springer spaniels. The kids were throwing a football back and forth, and the dogs were tussling with each other. I stopped, and waited. There was something poignant about the scene.

I felt as if I were watching the remnants of child-hood . . . the carefree days being played out before it was too late. Amy had only a light jacket on, and her hands were red with cold. Oblivious, she laughed as she ran to catch the ball, the dogs tripping her up. She fell in a heap with them bounding over her. Andy's voice rang out, calling the plays, his voice sounding now like his older brother's.

I shoved my hands deep into my pockets, shiver-ing. *What is this I'm feeling?* I wondered. Beyond them was our house, looking stately and patient, waiting for them with warm rooms and burning lamps. This house has watched three other children play in front of it . . . only for them to grow up and leave. And then I knew I was—*on the ragged edge.* By now, at middle age, a familiar place for me, but I still don't like it.

Being *on the edge* is when your children leave home for the first time. Or maybe it is having a parent that has forgotten your name. She still has the face of your mother—her voice, her smile—but now, *you* are the mother. Maybe it's after you leave a church that meant much to you, and your new place of worship is just not the same. Or perhaps it's moving to a new place, and you still don't know the "code words" to acceptance here. Or the feeling you have after you've left a job that was your life. Perhaps it is the loss of an important relationship, and while life is supposed to be going on by now, your heart is still torn. And you're waiting for life to begin again—to catch you up like a kite that finally gets a full, strong wind. But instead, you're just going through the motions. Plodding along the shoreline, following . . . where?

At this point of evaluation, you are not far from where you've poured your energies, your efforts—your heart—and so while you're standing back on the shore . . . watching . . . your heart is still out there, awash, getting bashed on the rocks, and nobody knows it but you. It is an awkward, lonely place to be. Loss—but not quite loss. This is the ragged edge. It is a place of waiting, of not knowing the outcome. It is a place of wondering, *How did I do, God? Did I follow You on that one?*

As I stood there watching my children, I thought about John the Baptist, imprisoned before Herod had him beheaded. He wondered, Is Jesus really the Messiah? Is what He is preaching true? Jesus sent word back to him, telling him of the wonderful miracles that were happening, and yes, it was all true. The kingdom was happening, and John was a part of it.

*R*ESULTS ARE GOD'S RESPONSIBILITY; OBEDIENCE IS OUR RESPONSIBILITY.

The *edge* is both a dangerous and a wonderful place to be. Dangerous because we know the effort, the energy, we have poured into a person, a relationship, a situation, and we want to know that our efforts have not been in vain. We want to see results, and while we wait for them, we are forced to confront what we've believed, what we've lived. Sometimes there's some serious cleanup to do at this place of midlife reevaluation.

So how do we respond when we're on the edge? Once our family was caught in a gale off the Washington coast. Our boat engine had quit, and the waves were pushing us toward jagged rocks. We panicked until the obvious solution occurred to us: *Put down your anchor!* We did, and were secured. Hebrews 6:19 says: "This hope [in God's promises] we have as an anchor of the soul, both sure and steadfast."

I watched my children go into the house and wondered how to tell them once again (so they'd listen): *"Look. There are only a few things that matter: Knowing God. Seeking out His truth in the Bible and living it. Loving others."* But I realize I've already done lots of telling, and maybe what I really want is "results," the assurance that I've done OK. But I need to let go of that desire. The fact is, results are God's business; obedience is mine.

Are you are on the "ragged edge" right now? Are you waiting to see the outcome of what you've invested? Sometimes it feels as if you're going to be in that place forever. Instead of settling into that place and "waiting" for the results, think about new ways to invest yourself in others. Is there someone who would especially benefit from your time, your daily prayer on her behalf, a weekly note of encouragement? Find new paths of obedience, and commit the results to God.

Father, the ragged edge is a difficult place to be. It's an ill-defined, uncertain place where we want to know that our hard work was worth it, that it meant something. Forgive our impatience, Lord. Keep our eyes from searching for results, and instead, open them to new opportunities for obedience. Help us to live an obedient life and leave the results to You. In Jesus' name, amen.

*Therefore, my beloved brethren, be steadfast, immovable, always
abounding in the work of the Lord, knowing that your labor is not in
vain.*

1 CORINTHIANS 15:58

LISTEN TO YOUR LIFE.

SEE IT FOR THE FATHOMLESS MYSTERY IT IS.

IN THE BOREDOM AND PAIN OF IT NO LESS THAN IN

THE EXCITEMENT AND GLADNESS;

TOUCH, TASTE, SMELL YOUR WAY TO THE HOLY

AND HIDDEN HEART OF IT BECAUSE IN THE LAST ANALYSIS

ALL MOMENTS ARE KEY MOMENTS, AND LIFE ITSELF IS GRACE.

Frederick Buechner, *Now and Then*

CHAPTER ELEVEN

Ribbons of Joy

How does one box up a life? We could no longer put off what was heartbreakingly inevitable. Because of our mother's deteriorating mental condition, my sisters, brothers, and I made the difficult decision to place our beautiful little mother in a foster home. She still doesn't seem old to us, only more and more like a little girl who is lost and confused, being slowly pulled from us by Alzheimer's. Without constant supervision, she wanders away.

Now it was our task to parcel out her things and close up her place. On a summer afternoon my sisters and I took seven big boxes—one for each of us children—and began sorting through the pictures, letters, and keepsakes.

There was no order to any of it. Mother's confused state of mind was evident from the chaos we found throughout the drawers and closets. Mother had gotten into her box of cherished Christmas decorations, collected over the years, and had strewn them throughout her apartment in odd, unexpected places: in the hutch, the bookcase, a kitchen drawer. She had taken a particular liking to red curling ribbon, and we found bits and pieces of it carefully placed on top of a dresser or in a cup in the kitchen.

Tucked in last month's Safeway circular I found an ardent love letter my father had written to her before they were married. My birth announcement was underneath her bed in a church bulletin. Mother had cut out all the pictures from old family albums (something she would have found horrifying had she been in her right mind). A tintype of Aunt Some-body-or-Other stared back at us from a pile of the grandchildren's current school photos. We sifted through hundreds of letters she'd saved—from college, from early in her marriage, and from my sister Janie, who spent twelve years as a missionary in the Far East.

Gradually we saw some order take shape. Like a kaleidoscope of decades of family relationships, the complete jumble began to portray her life. Flashes of *her*, reminders of the mother we knew, began to appear: a desk full of her writings; Bible study notes on the book of Revelation, from which she'd taught so many times; notebooks full of her thoughts and feelings; prayer journals; a book of favorite quotations; her diary (found in a kitchen drawer). Her life held much heartache and personal loss, but over and over she wrote, "How wonderful to know the love of Jesus!"

Then we'd open something else and find more red ribbon. "Crazy!" I laughed, as I found some in a bathroom drawer with her hair brushes. Tears filled my eyes. *What are you trying to say to us, Mother?* I mused. Those red ribbons must have seemed pretty, decorative, to her.

Back at home, where I'd been helping two of my children pack for college and our oldest son pack for a job in a distant city, I faced other boxes. I began to think they represented eras of our lives. Boxes of old maternity clothes, infant clothes and toys, baby books and grade school awards. Boxes of college textbooks; wedding veils and cake tops. Like

pieces of the puzzle, all part of the big picture—
a life.

Some things defy labeling, boxing up. How do I
"box up" my mother's smile that has permeated my
whole life? I can't. How do I box up children who
are the light of our lives? It's impossible.

WE CAN FIND JOY, EVEN IN TIMES
OF CONFUSION AND DIFFICULTY,
AS WE INVITE CHRIST INTO THOSE MOMENTS.

I wonder what Mary, the mother of Jesus, did with
the gifts the wise men had brought to her Son.
Maybe she boxed them up for a later time. Scripture
says that she "kept all these things and pondered
them in her heart." Over the years there was much
to come—the flight to Egypt, the trip back home, the
pilgrimage to Jerusalem when Jesus was twelve, years
spent in the carpenter shop, His first miracle when
he turned the water into wine. She knew He could
do it—He was the Father's Son. And she told the
servants, "Whatever He tells you to do—do it." They
used what was at hand. Common, ordinary water,
poured out in obedience to Him, became

uncommon wine—better than the first. The celebration continued, and joy reigned.

If I were to have a conversation with Mary, I think she would say, "Go ahead—invite Him to your 'marriage,' your life. Even if it seems like a disorganized mess and you have no 'wine' to offer." Then do what He says. Give Him the common, ordinary day. Poured out in obedience to Christ, the common moments will become uncommon, and you will find ribbons of joy, ribbons of celebration.

Have you run out of "wine"? Is the joy in your life crushed, smothered? The daily routines of life can drain us of joy. But like those seemingly misplaced red ribbons, even in the midst of confusing endings and beginnings, when Christ is invited in— there is joy.

Think about how you can invite Christ into the ordinary, commonplace moments of your days. Ponder what you can "pour out" in obedience to Him, and then look for the ribbons of joy in unexpected places.

Lord, You came to redeem our entire life, to give us abundant, overflowing joy. We say we want Your joy, but often we ask You to wait while we clean things up before inviting You in. Forgive us, Lord. We do invite You—right now—into the moments of our life, with our deficiencies, our busyness, our bad planning, our frustration. We want to obey You, Lord—to pour out what You give us so that others will be refreshed. In Jesus' name, amen.

But Mary kept all these things and pondered them in her heart.

LUKE 2:19

JOY IS REALLY A ROAD SIGN POINTING US TO GOD.

ONCE WE HAVE FOUND GOD . . .

WE NO LONGER NEED TO TROUBLE OURSELVES

SO MUCH ABOUT THE QUEST FOR JOY.

C. S. Lewis, *Surprised by Joy*

CHAPTER TWELVE

Leaving the Wilderness

I was flying home from a speaking engagement. It was a clear, crisp day, the visibility unusually good. I leaned my head against the window, drinking in the view. I was tired, and it felt good to relax. I thought of the people I had met on this trip. I had flown to this city on the other side of America, where I didn't know anyone. But during this short time, I had made some new friends. One woman in particular, a leader in her church and community, made an impression on me. She waited until everyone else had left after I finished speaking. Then she crumpled as she poured out her heart about the difficulties she was going through. Often a speaker is a "safe place" to tell secrets. As I listened, I was amazed again at the depth of pain in people's lives, their private agonies. I could tell that in spite of her outwardly put-together life, this woman was experiencing the loneliness and pain of the desert. I recognized it because I'd been there myself.

I looked down again. We had passed the Plains and were now over the Great Basin, mile upon mile of wilderness. It appeared to be flat, dry, and barren. *What brave souls would want to live here?* I wondered. And then, surprisingly, I saw little communities, a solitary house at the end of a road here and there. I wanted to shout down to them, "Hey! Why do you stay there?! Don't you know that only a thousand miles away are beautiful, fertile places, where things grow? Why settle here, where you're forced to eke out an existence? You just gotta get over those mountains. . . . Get out of that wilderness!" And I'm sure many of them would shout back, "Mind your own business—we like it here. It has its own beauty, you know!"

As I flew, I thought of Hagar, Sarah's handmaiden. She had given birth to Abraham's son, Ishmael. This was causing major problems and jealousies in the camp. Finally, Sarah insisted to Abraham that Hagar and Ishmael had to go (Genesis 21). In the wilderness, when Hagar and Ishmael were at the point of desperation and death, God saw their plight and sustained them with water from a well.

If we read further, Scripture tells us that Hagar *stayed* in the desert. She lived there, found a wife for Ishmael in Egypt, and died there. The Bible says that God was with Ishmael as he grew up in the wilderness.

As surely as there are times to go to the wilderness, there are also times to leave it and move on. How funny we humans are—we go kicking and screaming into the wilderness of pain or sickness—and then we grow accustomed to it and resist the idea of moving on. I think of Moses, escaping to the back side of the wilderness after he killed the Egyptian (Exodus 2). And Elijah, running to the desert to escape from Jezebel and Ahab (1 Kings 19). Jesus spent time in the wilderness preparing for His public ministry.

Some would avoid desert experiences at all cost, deny they exist, deny their validity. But desert experiences are valuable—indeed, they are an essential part of a fruitful life, where we hear God's voice and

He refreshes us while we are there. But the time will come—if we are committed to growth—when we will leave the wilderness.

THE DESERT IS A VALUABLE PLACE TO VISIT, BUT WE SHOULDN'T WANT TO LIVE THERE.

Not long ago I went alone to a favorite spot in the mountains. I packed a small can of juice and some crackers in my jacket pocket and began to hike off the dirt road. The mountains stretched off in the distance, their snowcapped peaks against the blue sky breathtaking in their beauty. I found an old tree stump. There I set out the crackers and the juice, sang a hymn of the Cross, and had a private Communion service. As I prayed, I considered a burden I'd often relinquished but had gone back and picked up again. I was sensing it was time to "leave that wilderness." I wrote out the burden, rolled up the little piece of paper, and slipped it inside the tree stump. This time when I left it with Him, I didn't look back. Paul Tournier wrote: "Life and faith always insist on moving forward—and I cannot move forward without leaving something behind . . . and possibly the most difficult to let go are treasuries of painful experiences."

When it is time to move on, it is time for reconciliation to imperfections, time for forgiveness, time to stop being a victim, time to take responsibility for where I am, who I am. Time to stop being enamored by, consumed by, the austere beauty of the desert. "Forgetting the things that are behind, I press on" (Philippians 3:13).

And to where do we move on? To the place where you can once again pick up the towel of servanthood, risk following God, stretch your faith. Only this time you move on armed with lessons you have learned in the wilderness.

Have you spent time in the desert recently? Are you there now? If so, what have you learned? Have you learned the value of the desert? Prayerfully consider whether it might be time for you to leave that place and move on. It may help you to record the lessons you have learned there and then write some "spiritual goals" for yourself. Put them in a sealed envelope, and tuck them away somewhere to be opened and reviewed at a later date. Remember that spiritual growth may require preparation time in the desert, but it also requires that we follow God's leading out of the desert and use what He has taught us to encourage others.

Lord, our life is truly a pilgrimage with You! Sometimes You lead us to beautiful, sunny places and sometimes to a desolate wilderness, where it's hard to understand what You're doing. But, Lord, we can trust Your goodness. Give us courage to follow You out of the desert and into new places of victory and provision. Keep us from becoming too comfortable in the desert so that when You call us, we are ready to move. In Jesus' name, amen.

To everything there is a season,
a time for every purpose under heaven.

ECCLESIASTES 3:1

WHAT QUICKENS MY PULSE NOW IS THE STRETCH AHEAD
RATHER THAN THE ONE BEHIND, AND IT IS MAINLY FOR
SOME CLUE AS TO WHERE I AM GOING THAT I SEARCH
THROUGH WHERE I HAVE BEEN, FOR SOME HINT AS TO
WHO I AM BECOMING OR FAILING TO BECOME THAT
I DELVE INTO WHAT USED TO BE.

Frederick Buechner, *The Sacred Journey*

CHAPTER THIRTEEN

The Care and Feeding of Dreams

I've had lots of dreams. I still do. Not the middle-of-the-night kind, but the kind that beckons like a lovely vision out on the horizon.

I vividly remember one night when I was twelve. I huddled before the furnace in my long flannel nightgown and thought, *Wouldn't it be great if someday I meet the man of my dreams? And we marry and have four or five children? And work for God somewhere . . . Somehow help people . . . help children . . . ?* Now, thirty-three years later, I recall that night and smile with wonder. God has given me a caring husband, four sons, one daughter, and opportunities to help people.

Some dreams are easier to realize than others. Some dreams take longer. As far back as I can remember, I have dreamed of writing. *Someday*, the longing deep inside of me always said, *I'll be a writer*. All through school, into college, and into marriage I kept diaries and journals. Then I quit. The early years of marriage were hectic, and my dream got shelved . . . until one night. We had just moved with our two small sons. Bill was at a meeting, the babies were both asleep, and I was sorting through boxes, putting things away. That's when I came across my journals, an odd assortment of notebooks and diaries in the bottom of a box. I remember hugging them to myself like long-lost children, crying, "Where have you been? I've missed you so!" It was like finding my "self" again. I sometimes felt that my soul had oozed out through my fingertips into the diaper pail or the dishwater. But here was concrete evidence that I had a self, and part of that self was this dream. I began journaling again, feeding the dream.

There have been other dreams. I remember ten years ago seeing a street person, a young woman. The look on her face shook me; the deadness, the blank expression. *She is lost,* I heard His still, small voice say. *Lost.* It was a vivid, electric moment. I wondered, *How do I reach that woman for Christ?* I could not get her face out of my mind. That experience became part of the impetus for my dream of a ministry to women in prison.

I've pursued some dreams I shouldn't have. When we became pastors of a church, I discovered that the previous pastor's wife, a gifted woman, had developed an effective outreach for women in the community. Not waiting to see if this was something God wanted me to do, I plunged in, carrying on her dream. To my dismay, the outreaches under my direction fizzled. Flopped. I felt like a failure and wondered what I had done wrong. Later, I realized that taking on her ministry wasn't "me"— it wasn't *my* dream. I did it because it was a good idea, because it worked for her, and because I thought others expected it of me. Humbled, I began a Bible study with two other women, which, to my surprise, thrived and became a successful ministry of the church.

 *E*VEN IF YOU CAN'T FULLY REALIZE
YOUR DREAM NOW,
YOU CAN FEED IT.

At times my dreams were frustrated, delayed, or reshaped, as when my children were small. I wondered then, *Will I ever be a writer?* It seemed impossible. And yet the crucible of family life was so necessary, for there I learned the best lessons in trust . . . in timing . . . in what is most essential for right now. I didn't need to abandon my dream. I could put some energy into feeding it for the future, knowing that I needed to wait until later to see it realized. I've learned that if God has given me the dream—if it is truly from Him—then, in His timing, I can proceed.

Dreams aren't always huge, lofty goals. Sometimes they are hopes and wishes that keep us growing, developing. I remember watching how easily a close friend used her gifts of hospitality and homemaking. *I would love to do that, too,* I thought. And as I watched her, I was able to grow in that area.

The thing about dreams is that they are "safe." It is one thing to have a dream—it is quite another to actually work to realize that dream. I weighed my dream of writing. Was God in this dream? I believed so. But the thought of actually writing, of struggling to make that dream a reality, was frightening. It still is. I'm often tempted to believe the negative: *Awfully big giants out there. There's no way I can do this.* Fear is powerful, and it often drowns out the voice of faith. Past failure can keep you from using the gifts God has given you. But if God has given you a dream and you are willing to feed it, He will lead you as you work toward that vision that beckons on the horizon.

What are your dreams? Can you list them on a sheet of paper? Are you able to work on realizing them right now? If not, are they sitting in the bottom of a box? Don't let them die for lack of food. Maybe it's time for you to give attention to a talent long buried. Remember that you are a steward of the dreams God has given you. If you invest time in feeding them now, your dreams will continue to live until, in God's timing, He brings them to fruition.

Lord, there is so much that You want to do through us if we will only look at our dreams with eyes of faith. Thank You for the unique and varied gifts that You give to each one of us. We pray that we will be faithful stewards of them. Help us to exercise the necessary discipline and patience to refine our dreams, to feed them, and to work toward realizing them, in Your timing, and for the sake of Your kingdom. In Christ's name, amen.

Where there is no vision, the people perish.

PROVERBS 29:18, KJV

CHERISH YOUR VISIONS; CHERISH YOUR IDEALS;
CHERISH THE MUSIC THAT STIRS IN YOUR HEART,
THE BEAUTY THAT FORMS IN YOUR MIND, THE LOVELINESS
THAT DRAPES YOUR PUREST THOUGHTS, FOR OUT OF THEM
WILL GROW ALL DELIGHTFUL CONDITIONS. . . . "ASK AND YOU
SHALL RECEIVE." DREAM LOFTY DREAMS, AND AS YOU DREAM,
SO SHALL YOU BECOME. . . . THE GREATEST ACHIEVEMENT
WAS AT FIRST AND FOR A TIME A DREAM. THE OAK SLEEPS IN
THE ACORN; THE BIRD WAITS IN THE EGG; AND IN THE
HIGHEST VISION OF THE SOUL A WAKING ANGEL STIRS.
DREAMS ARE THE SEEDLINGS OF REALITIES.

James Allen, *As a Man Thinketh*

CHAPTER FOURTEEN

Unquenchable Love

I suppose that the process of losing Mother was so painful that I carefully packaged the pain away into the box of sympathy cards, clippings, and remembrances. Now, six months later, I reluctantly took out the box. Her birthday, Thanksgiving, and Christmas had all passed without her for the first time.

As I thought of her, it seemed impossible to me that someone as vibrant, as lovely, as my mother could be gone. I know about heaven, and I cling to that blessed hope. But what about *her,* the essence of who she was, what she was to me and to the rest of her family? As I sorted through the memories, I tried to forget the lingering, debilitating illness and instead tried to burn into my memory her voice, her laughter, and the dancing brown eyes that saw humor in unexpected places. But I tried in vain, and I began to worry that I would lose her, even here, in my memory. The sorrow was hardening into an unrecognizable, empty place. I wondered, *When you lose someone you love—someone who loves you—what happens to the love? Where does it go?*

Last night I dreamed that Eric and Chris, two of our sons who are both away at college, could not get home for a family celebration. I was distraught, and in my dream insisted, "They've *got* to be here. Everyone else is here, and we need them." So somehow we got them both on the telephone and told them to open their gifts the same time we opened ours— on the phone together. It helped a little, but not entirely. I wanted them with me—Eric's lankiness, his easygoing "How ya doin', Ma?" Chris, sitting at the kitchen counter while he ate cold cereal and told me about his classes and friends. I wanted *them,* not memories. I awoke feeling hollow.

The temptation is to carefully protect the vestiges of security—old friends, extended family—and become a curator of the family museum, to plan and live for when the children are home. Only most of them aren't children anymore; they're men, with places to go and people to see. Home is now a refueling base for three of our five children, an occasional stopover on their way to life.

Sometimes in the cold ashes of our losses, we have trouble seeing "the living." When certain women came to the empty tomb bringing spices, two angels said to them, "Why do you seek the living among the dead?" (Luke 24:5). And as Jesus walked along the road to Emmaus with two of His followers, they did not recognize Him (Luke 24:16). It was only later that they were amazed at how they had not known who He was: "Did not our heart burn within us while He talked with us on the road, and while He opened the Scriptures to us?" (v. 32).

The disciples could have continued to be consumed with the horror of the Cross. Later, they could have simply remained awestruck by the Resurrection and done nothing except sit and enjoy Jesus' presence with them. Instead, after that, Jesus *left them*. It was into that emptiness that the Holy Spirit came, comforting them and empowering them for ministry.

*I*N THE EMPTINESS OF LOSS, LOVE DOESN'T DIE;
IT JUST CHANGES AND GROWS.

I remember hearing Mother tell about when she
became a Christian. She came to accept Jesus fifty-five
years ago—no casual side-trip for her. As a young,
single mother desperately in need of meaning, she
plunged headlong, wholeheartedly into following
Christ, her life radically turned upside down. She
got, as they say, *saved.* In this box of memories, I find
Mother's journal. An entry made late one Saturday
night reads: "We're harvesting, and so we're busy.
Awfully tired tonight, and I have yet to 'get' my
Sunday school lesson. I need to more than 'get' it.
It must 'get' me! Wonderful to know the love of Jesus
. . . !" The message did "get" her. Mother never quite
got over the wonder of knowing Jesus and burned
with longing that others would know Him, too. I see
now that her very life was a gift to those who loved her,
and out of the broken life she offered to Him, He
made something beautiful and fruitful.

I got a call from Eric and Chris today. They can't
come home for break this year. It's too far away, and
they don't have enough time. But Eric is going to fix

a nice dinner at his apartment, and he wondered how to cook a turkey. They want to invite some guys in, they said, who also can't get home. I smiled as I passed along some recipes and realized that they were originally my mother's and Bill's mother's. Love doesn't die; it just changes and grows.

It is as we give out of our own emptiness and loss that Christ, the all-sufficient one, restores our joy. All that we have been given—the good and the bad— are gifts to us. Through the inevitable changes of life, there may be some empty places at our table, but then new faces come. And His love—that love that never leaves us—is still here.

Think about a time of "emptiness" or loss in your life. If you experienced Christ's comfort in that painful time, what was that like for you? You might want to share your experience with others who are facing loss. If you are walking that path right now, consider offering your emptiness as a sacrifice to God, and ask Him to create something fruitful from it.

Lord, in this life, loss is inevitable. Sometimes we feel it so keenly that we wonder how we can go on. But as You opened the eyes of Your followers in Emmaus, they were comforted and encouraged. And so we ask You to reveal Yourself to us in the midst of our own losses. Into our emptiness, pour Your comfort. And make of our brokenness something beautiful as we sacrifice it to You. In Jesus' name, amen.

Love is as strong as death. . . .
Many waters cannot quench love, nor can the floods drown it.
SONG OF SOLOMON 8:6-7

WHAT WONDERS GOD HAS DONE WITH NOTHINGNESS.

Mother Teresa, *Blessed Are You: Mother Teresa and the Beatitudes*

CHAPTER FIFTEEN

Encouragement: A Gift from the Heart

*I*t was Monday morning, and I sat on the couch in my robe, feeling swamped. Not so much by the big challenges as by the "chronicness" of life. Phone calls I needed to make. Bills. The dirty house. Writing deadlines. Projects that needed attention. Family relationships that seemed to circle around the same arguments, the same difficulties. *Laundry . . . .* I stared at the huge pile of socks before me. Laundry seemed representative of my life somehow. As I sorted socks, I thought, *It's always the same old "stuff" that needs tending.*

All of us have some of that "same old stuff"—

chronic, routine things that need ongoing attention. And we need help at times just to keep going, to face another day. Sometimes we need an extra boost from someone who will say, "Keep going—you can make it!" In a word, we need encouragement.

Encouragement is a gift from the heart. When we offer encouragement, we give someone some of our courage, our strength. The ongoing, routine things of life can drain us, and we all need someone to comfort us, to share the load, to urge us forward. Encouragement is a wonderful gift, but it doesn't cost much—just a word or two, a smile, a sensitive, generous heart.

Seventeen years ago Bill was speaking at a convention on parenting while I was trying to manage our three unruly little sons in the back of the auditorium. We were tired, and I was on the verge of tears, wishing I was at home. At that moment an elderly pastor sat down near me. "You remind me of my wife when we were young," he said. "She always had to take care of the kids in church. But you know what?" He leaned closer, his eyes bright. "We raised eight of the greatest kids. We love them so much! Don't worry about having to do everything right. Just love them; they'll be fine." He got up and left, never knowing that at that moment his words were *life* to me.

Four years ago, struggling with chronic pain, I found myself once again in the doctor's office, crying, "I am so tired of pain! How do I go on?"

My doctor said kindly, "I *do* see progress. You're just in a little dip right now. Don't be discouraged—keep on."

I doggedly stuck to the exercise regime, the therapy, and sure enough, I am enjoying health. When I needed them most, the doctor's kind words inspired me to keep on.

There have been times when I've sat down to write, and I've prayed, *Lord, show me what to write. I have nothing to give.* An idea comes, and then later I receive an encouraging note from a reader who says, "That was just what I needed to hear." These letters remind me of Proverbs 25:25: "As cold water to a weary soul, so is good news from a far country."

*E*NCOURAGEMENT IS A GIFT THAT
KEEPS ON GIVING.

When we encourage others in their neediest moments (and sometimes we are unaware of just how deep the need is), we offer them a lifeline, something to hold on to when the waves of life threaten to knock us down. Proverbs 18:21 says: "Death and life are in the power of the tongue, and those who love it will eat its fruit." Think of it: You can literally offer someone *life* by an encouraging word, a smile, or taking a moment to try to understand what she's going through. A phone call and a sincere "How are you—really?" can be so simple, yet so important.

Think of a time when someone encouraged you. Do you remember the impact it had? What did that person do? Did she write a note, make a phone call, offer a listening ear over a cup of coffee or tea, clean your bathroom, watch your kids? No doubt someone in your life needs encouragement right now. It may be a coworker, a member of your own family, or someone you see on a daily basis. Try to imagine the unique pressures he or she is facing, and prayerfully look for opportunities to offer encouragement.

Lord, thank You for those times when Your Spirit has spoken words of comfort, wisdom, and encouragement to our hearts through one of Your people. Teach us to look beyond our own chronic, ordinary problems to see the needs of others. Remind us, Lord, that "death and life are in the power of the tongue." May our words be life to those in need of encouragement. Amen.

Anxiety in the heart of man causes depression, but a good word makes it glad.

PROVERBS 12:25

IF I AM INCONSIDERATE ABOUT THE COMFORT OF OTHERS,
OR THEIR FEELINGS, OR EVEN THEIR LITTLE WEAKNESSES;
IF I AM CARELESS ABOUT THEIR LITTLE HURTS AND MISS
OPPORTUNITIES TO SMOOTH THEIR WAY . . .
THEN I KNOW NOTHING OF CALVARY LOVE.

Amy Carmichael, *If*

CHAPTER SIXTEEN

Seeing the Glory

I don't demand to see the miraculous—I would not dare. God does not show His glory at our whim. But sometimes I get the feeling I'm in the middle of the desert—already out of Egypt but not yet to the Promised Land. Then I wonder, *Is His presence really among us?*

I remind myself that this is a faith walk, so naturally the view through the glass is cloudy at times. We study our Bibles; we listen to sermons. We pray; we encourage one another. But I long to know that in all of that, He is present, that it is truly He—the Holy One—whom we worship. I think of Moses, after he came down from the glorious meeting with God on the mountaintop, only to discover that his people had already become involved in idol worship.

Later, Moses encountered God with this poignant plea: "You say to me, 'Bring up this people.' But You have not let me know whom You will send with me" (Exodus 33:12). Moses also expressed a desire to know that God was present with him when he said to God, "If Your Presence does not go with us, do not bring us up from here" (v. 15). Sometimes I feel like Moses as I pray, "If Your presence doesn't go with me, don't take me any farther."

But once in a rare while . . . God unexpectedly lifts the veil just a bit and gives us a wondrous moment that assures us of His presence with us. And we ponder it later, as Mary the mother of Jesus did after the wise men had left. We don't share the experience with just anyone, but around a table with close friends, or on the edge of the bed with our children gathered around us, we tell the story.

It was almost twenty years ago. Jon was six, Eric, four, and Chris, two. The next day was Jon's first day at school. He was excited; I was filled with dread. How could I entrust this precious child to strangers? I tried not to show my own fear, because Jon was nervous about riding the school bus. I already envisioned how he'd look the next morning: new jeans and navy blue windbreaker, his pink name tag around his neck, his white blond hair neatly combed, looking for all the world like a lamb being led to slaughter. . I wondered, *Whose idea was it to have pink name tags, anyway? Older boys might tease him.*

I sat on the floor in the boys' bedroom to pray with them before they went to sleep. "Boys," I told them—more for my sake than for theirs—"remember, you have guardian angels. The Bible says that the angel of the Lord camps around those that fear Him and that God gives His angels charge over us, to keep us in all our ways. We can't see them because they're invisible. But they're very real. In fact, I saw my guardian angel once."

"You did?" I had their attention.

*G*OD GIVES US GLIMPSES OF HIMSELF IN THE MOST UNEXPECTED PLACES.

I awoke one night when I was about nine years old to see someone sitting on my bed. I knew instinctively he was an angel. I stared at him, this awesome-looking creature, with a full, curly head of hair and a flowing robe. I lay frozen, staring in fascinated terror. My mother always left the stove light on in the kitchen, which provided a night-light that came through to the bedrooms. In the soft light I could see him plainly. He was as real as my two sisters, who were sleeping soundly in the same room with me. I breathed shallowly, not wanting him to know I was awake. Then he turned his head and looked at me. I immediately closed my eyes, pretending to be asleep. And I did go to sleep. When I told my family the next morning, they nodded and smiled, but I think they thought I had been dreaming. I wasn't. The encounter is still real and vivid to me.

I finished telling the story, and just as I was tucking the boys in, Bill came in from a meeting at the church. He poked his head in the bedroom. "I've got a surprise for you guys." He held three large, ornately decorated angel cookies, one for each of them. "A nice lady in the church made these for you."

Angel cookies? Why would she make angel cookies for our sons in September?

Jon quickly offered his assessment. "Hey, God is saying, 'You really do have guardian angels!'" Now, years later, I ponder that tangible reminder of God's presence in our lives. I think of how often I've prayed for God's protection and then seen how He has kept us. Those reminders of God's faithfulness in the past help us to remember that God is with us today . . . wherever we are.

If you have experienced an unusual evidence of God's presence, thank God for the way He has increased your faith through it. But remember that God is with us, even when we don't feel His presence in an extraordinary way. Spend some time thinking about God's faithfulness to you in the past. In what ways can you choose to trust God for today and for tomorrow? Ask God to open your eyes to how intimately He cares for you.

 Oh, God, thank You for Your abiding presence with us. Whatever the cost, may we dwell in Your presence, the ultimate safe place. Whether we feel Your presence or not, help us to trust what Your Word tells us about Your care for Your people. May we find comfort in the knowledge that You shelter us in the cleft of the rock and cover us with Your mighty hand. In Jesus' name, amen.

Eye has not seen, nor ear heard, nor have entered into the heart of man the things which God has prepared for those who love Him.

1 CORINTHIANS 2:9

THE GREAT LACK OF OUR RELIGION IS, WE DO NOT KNOW GOD. THE ANSWER TO EVERY COMPLAINT OF FEEBLENESS AND FAILURE, THE MESSAGE TO EVERY CONGREGATION OR CONVENTION SEEKING INSTRUCTION ON HOLINESS OUGHT TO BE SIMPLY, WHAT IS THE MATTER: HAVE YOU NOT GOD? IF YOU REALLY BELIEVE IN GOD, HE WILL PUT ALL RIGHT.

Andrew Murray, *Waiting On God*

CHAPTER SEVENTEEN

Awesome New Places

*I*t has been quite a transition for our Amy, going into seventh grade this year. I went to her open house; sat bunched down into a too-small chair; and watched Mrs. Biesman, her math teacher, write mysterious things on the chalkboard. I pretended to be adult and wise, hoping I wouldn't blow my cover and be discovered as the math illiterate I really am. *How in the world is Amy going to get this,* I wondered. *If she did, it would certainly be in spite of my help!* The math was daunting enough, even not taking into account Amy's learning disabilities and her less-than-helpful mother. That morning Amy had stormed at breakfast, "I hate math! I just don't get it!"

I sat up just in time to hear Mrs. Biesman say, "I tell my students if they are feeling lost, uncomfortable, or confused, they are in the perfect place to learn something new."

The perfect place to learn something new . . . I guess that's where I am, I thought. These days I feel as if *I* am in a new school, with a lot of new "classes." I am now a mother-in-law, and I pray, "Lord, show me what Brittni needs from me." I wonder, too, how to mother growing-up sons, after hearing long distance that Eric has severe food allergies and needs to drastically change his diet. How much is his responsibility, and where should I help? I'm often not sure when to pray, when to shut up, or when to speak up.

I took on the challenge of being a magazine editor, another new hat for me—a wonderful, fulfilling challenge, but it puts me in a place where it is easy to feel overwhelmed. I sit at my desk and pray, *God, I really want to follow You, to obey You in these new avenues of my life.* I feel for all the world like Amy on her first day of math class. What do I really know about following God here?

When Jacob left his family and home, he was afraid for his life. He was a fugitive, and his brother had vowed to kill him. He spent the night out in the middle of nowhere, a stone for his pillow (Genesis 28). He must have felt isolated and overwhelmed. He had promise of an inheritance and a blessing (which he'd deceived his brother, Esau, to get), but things didn't look very promising. And yet as Jacob slept, he dreamed and saw a ladder that extended from heaven to earth, and angels of God were ascending and descending. The Lord told him, "I am with you and will keep you wherever you go" (v. 15).

As I grow into new areas, I am learning important things about following God. He is teaching me that in my *"inability,"* He is able. He is also teaching me not to be afraid of my own weaknesses and insecurities, because I am learning, too, that if He calls me, He will equip me: "The Lord will perfect that which concerns me" (Psalm 138:8).

In math, one concept builds on another. Growth is like that. It is an unfolding process as God guides me step-by-step, experience by experience, through uncomfortable times—times when I feel I'm in way over my head.

WHEN GOD THRUSTS US OUT OF OUR
COMFORT ZONE, HE PROVES
HIS ABILITY IN OUR PLACE OF INABILITY.

I used to believe that if I were totally obedient to God, He would call me to the far reaches of the world—and He has that option. But I'm immensely relieved to see that God begins with us exactly where we are. Not long ago I was praying, "Lord, I'll go wherever You lead, do whatever You ask, in the neediest place ever!"

And it seemed the Lord said in His still, small voice: *That place is right where you are—in the opportunities that come to you every day, the challenges of life. Write honestly about what God is doing in your life. Love and support your husband where he is. Be compassionate with Amy. Go the extra mile with your coworker. Build bridges in the kingdom. Share My love with your neighbor.* The new mission fields He calls me to are really adventures of the spirit—opening doors of my life and inviting Him in more and more, right where I live. And I can grow from there.

Last week Amy came home from school, glowing. She'd received the "Student of the Month" award in math class! It was as if she'd won the Nobel prize, and now she's decided she really likes math. The things that are so daunting and difficult to learn can turn out to be wonderful and satisfying.

Are you facing a new situation? Is God thrusting you out of your comfort zone? Can you think of ways in which God has demonstrated His sufficiency—His ability—when you have felt your own inability? In every new situation, every "discomfort zone," we have the opportunity to seek God's comfort and guidance. Commit to trusting Him in each new area of growth. Remember, He is there, and you can open yourself up to Him right where you are and enter an adventure of new challenges with Him. I believe you will be delighted and surprised to discover that God is present in each new lonely, strange place into which you venture.

 Lord, thank You for new opportunities and challenges that stretch us. They can be frightening, and often we feel overwhelmed and inadequate. And yet in those new places You prove Yourself faithful and loving to us, Your children. May we learn to welcome these new opportunities and then grow into all that You want us to be. In Christ's name, amen.

Jacob awoke from his sleep and said, "Surely the Lord is in this place, and I did not know it."

GENESIS 28:16

IF WE COULD SEE BENEATH THE SURFACE OF MANY A LIFE, WE WOULD SEE THAT THOUSANDS OF PEOPLE WITHIN THE CHURCH ARE SUFFERING SPIRITUALLY FROM "ARRESTED DEVELOPMENT"; THEY NEVER REACH SPIRITUAL MATURITY; THEY NEVER DO ALL THE GOOD THEY WERE INTENDED TO DO; AND THIS IS DUE TO THE FACT THAT AT SOME POINT IN THEIR LIVES THEY REFUSED TO GO FURTHER; SOME ACT OF SELF-SACRIFICE WAS REQUIRED OF THEM, AND THEY FELT THEY COULD NOT AND WOULD NOT MAKE IT; SOME HABITS HAD TO BE GIVEN UP, SOME PERSONAL RELATION ALTERED AND RENOUNCED, AND THEY REFUSED TO TAKE THE ONE STEP WHICH WOULD HAVE OPENED UP FOR THEM A NEW AND VITAL DEVELOPMENT.

Olive Wyon, *Into His Presence: Spiritual Disciplines for the Inner Life*

CHAPTER EIGHTEEN

Careful Walking

*I*t was our last day of vacation boating in the San Juan Islands off the Washington coast. But school started in a few days, and we were ready to go home. Bill angled the boat toward the dock, and being a good first mate, I poised to jump off and tie up.

As I stepped off the boat, my foot slipped, and I kept going, falling into the cold ocean. I remember it as if it were a dream in slow motion and I were watching it happen to someone else. One thought was uppermost in my mind—avoid hitting the prop. I grabbed onto a railing of the boat as it slammed me against the dock, and somehow Bill and the kids got the boat stopped and helped me clamber onto the dock, where I lay moaning in pain. I had bruises and scrapes, and later, X rays showed a fractured and dislocated shoulder. The doctor said he'd seen only one other person with an injury like this—a rodeo rider who'd been bucked off a bronco!

After surgery and months of physical therapy, I was better, almost as good as new. And then on a speaking trip, I lifted a box of books the wrong way. Suddenly the pain was back, gripping me in its vise and affecting my neck, arm, and shoulder. Back to physical therapy I went, the doctor again mentioning the possibility of surgery. The physical therapist told me that besides the fact that I was lifting things incorrectly, my posture was poor. I hadn't been holding my head straight, and even moving my head forward a couple of inches added extra pounds of stress to my frame.

Not long ago I was struggling again with another "old wound"—that of trying to earn acceptance by works. God and I have discussed this old wound many times. Setbacks can be discouraging, and I was angry at finding myself in this place again. *God,* I inwardly raged. *I gave that to You, remember? I left it at the Cross. Now here it is again, trying to defeat me! What's the deal?*

An insight from Scripture shed some light. The book of Joshua, in chapters 6 through 8, tells the story of the Israelites' triumphant march across the Jordan into the Promised Land and the great victory at Jericho. And then as they went on to Ai—an insignificant little city—they were defeated. Whipped. Joshua was humiliated by this turn of events. "Why, God?" he asked.

Later it was discovered that Achan, of the tribe of Judah, had disobeyed God—he'd kept some pagan treasures and money and had hidden them in his tent. His disobedience carried enormous consequences for all of Israel. Years before in the wilderness, the children of Israel had had to learn painful lessons about obedience. And yet here they were, defeated again—even after entering the Promised Land.

It's important to pay attention to how you walk when you have old wounds. We needn't be held hostage by our past hurts, but it is essential that we be aware of the struggles that easily beset us. Wounds do heal, but the Great Physician must first perform surgery, dig out the "impurities," so that the wounds heal properly. Then, once we know our vulnerabilities, we are able to walk in obedience to God's Word.

*I*T'S IMPORTANT TO PAY ATTENTION TO HOW YOU WALK WHEN YOU HAVE OLD WOUNDS.

I have a friend who is unhappy in her marriage and is contemplating finding sweet release in the arms of another. She is at a critical point, and I long for her to know that the path she is contemplating is illusory. She knows what is right, but she must get to the point where she can turn and say, "Wait. Yes, there's a wound here, but God promised to meet my every need according to His riches in glory. I choose to allow *Him* to meet my needs."

Make no mistake—it is painful to make that choice. But when we say, "Not my will, but Yours," God does meet us there. And instead of this place of temptation being a place of defeat—as it was for Joshua at Ai—it can be a place of victory. Walking with an awareness of our past wounds actually makes us stronger and more able to compassion- ately minister God's grace to others in vulnerable places.

The things that we allow into our life in disobedi- ence to God's Word, things such as materialism, success, substance abuse, or, in my case, relying on performance to make me acceptable to God and to others, can defeat us. As I look back, I realize that on trips I often took along bulging briefcases, heavy bags. It was a habit, my carrying too much. I rationalized, "You never know, I might need this." Even on our vacation on the boat I had my ever present bag of books, manuscripts, and writing materials.

"Do you have to take all this stuff?" Bill asked. The same thinking—*that I'm not enough*—causes me to cram too much into my life. And, of course, I'm *not* enough, but He can be—to you and to me—if we ask Him to be.

Do you have an old wound? Perhaps it shows up in anger, anxiety, or guilt. Perhaps it's an addiction that has gotten you down more than once. It has often been said that our greatest strength, taken to extreme, can become our greatest weakness. Whatever our "pet sins"—the ones we are so reluctant to admit to, to part with—for complete healing we must allow God's light of truth into this most private part of our lives and seek His grace to cleanse and restore us. The first step is admitting the truth about what is at the core of our lives. The truth—although painful—sets us free.

I wish I could say I have learned all the lessons I need to know about what it means to not carry more than I should, both literally and figuratively. But maybe it's enough to know that I am learning to walk with an awareness of that old wound. I'm grateful that God loves us enough to speak His truth into our lives through ordinary and extraordinary ways—often through pain. He will do that for you, too, if you simply open your eyes and ears to see and hear what He is saying to you. After all, He is the Great Physician, and He came, as Isaiah said, "to heal the brokenhearted, to proclaim liberty to the captives and the opening of the prison to those who are bound . . . to comfort all who mourn . . . to give them beauty for ashes, the oil of joy for mourning, the garment of praise for the spirit of heaviness" (61:1-3).

Lord, Thank You for Your grace and mercy that continue to pursue us even when we forget what You've done for us in the past. Forgive us for slipping back into old ways of coping that seem comfortable to us yet are not Your will. Thank You for taking the time to clean out the impurities, even though the process may be painful. Help us to walk in newness of life. Lord, Your faithful Word keeps and protects us. Shine the light of Your truth on our inner selves, and set us free. In Jesus' name, amen.

*See then that you walk circumspectly,
not as fools but as wise.*

EPHESIANS 5:15

Oftentimes great and open temptations are the most harmless because they come with banners flying and bands playing and all the munitions of war in full view, so that we know we are in the midst of enemies that mean us damage, and we get ready to meet and resist them. Our peculiar dangers are those which surprise us and work treachery in our fort.

Henry Ward Beecher, quoted in *Treasury of Christian Faith*

CHAPTER NINETEEN

Faith of My Father

I close my eyes and remember what it was like to be twelve years old in the month of May. Sunlight streamed into the one-room schoolhouse as I tried to keep my mind on my book. Through the open window I heard the faraway drone of my father's tractor as he plowed, getting the ground ready for planting the spring crop. The winter had been long and harsh as storms swept across the rolling wheat fields of northern Montana. But in May, the Rocky Mountains off to the west somehow looked closer and gentler, and the glaciers glistened with fresh snow. The leaves on the trees of the schoolhouse began to leaf out, and dandelions brought cheery splashes of yellow.

On Saturdays in May, Dad would enlist my brother, my sister, and me to go with him to the field to pick up the biggest rocks so that the soil would be ready for the wheat he would soon plant. As I bounced along on the flatbed of the truck, I wondered about how those rocks kept turning up in our field. Every year we would haul them off of the field, but the next year we would find more rocks. Where did they come from?

Spring plowing—summer fallowing we called it—was dirty business. Dad would come in from the field covered with dirt, but he was always happy. He seemed to have a special feeling about spring plowing—the breaking up of the hard ground, the preparation of the soil to receive the seed. Spring meant promise, hope. Spring meant he would forget last year's drought or the hail that wiped out the winter wheat. Spring meant a new chance at harvest.

Today, as I think back to those days in the field with my dad, a hint of spring is in the air. I sit in my favorite place on a bench outside my front door and wait to leave with my husband to speak at a family conference. I feel reluctant to leave, and I cherish my home.

Just hours ago my daughter, Amy, and I gave each other little gifts to remind each of us of our love for the other. It helps us while we are apart. She lent me her teddy bear angel, and I lent her my mother's small Bible to keep next to her bed until I return home. Just before I gave it to her, I read what my dad had written to my mom in the flyleaf: "To my beloved wife, Harriet. You are the light of the world. A city that is set on a hill cannot be hid." Dad's angular writing with a blue fountain pen leaps out at me, and it seems as if his words are meant for me, too.

Dad was a man of few words. He found it difficult to talk about his deep love of God, family, and the land. But he lived out his faith for us. Every morning before my siblings and I left for school, he would read the King James Version of the Bible to us. He liked the psalms: "I will lift up mine eyes unto the hills, from whence cometh my help. My help cometh from the Lord, which made heaven and earth" (Psalm 121:1-2, KJV). My dad felt closest to God when he was out in the field, looking toward the mountains. When we moved to Oregon, he felt hemmed in by all the trees. "I like to see," he would say.

*B*REAKING UP THE FALLOW GROUND OF OUR LIVES IS ESSENTIAL TO BECOMING A PLACE WHERE SEEDS CAN GROW.

My father's life provided a rich soil for my faith to grow, and I am grateful. Yes, his life had "rocks"— those fallen, human parts that keep coming to the surface. In his own way he tried to remove the obstacles that prevented growth in his life. He suffered great losses, but he bore them with grace and dignity. For him, the best solutions for sorrow were to help someone else and to saturate his brokenness in God's Word.

We are our own soil, there is no doubt about that. You and I also have troublesome rocks that seem to come to the surface of our lives and prevent growth. The rocks may be our anxieties, difficult relationships, our selfishness, or any number of other obstacles. Like the farmer, we need to be willing to break up the fallow ground. For me, that sometimes means disturbing my life, turning over my assumptions about how God works, about my place in His field. I need to come once again to a place of receptivity, where the Word of God can take root in my

life and grow. I need to be tender, fresh, giving God
a place to express His will for me. Like spring plowing, this process can be messy. Sometimes it is very
hard, but without it, I will not be a place where
God's seed can grow.

Becoming a receptive place for seed to grow isn't
a onetime thing; it must be done seasonally for
continued harvests. For instance, at this season of
my life, it is difficult for me to leave home. I feel
disturbed by it. I would rather stay where it is comfortable. But I choose to see that God is breaking
up the rocks in my life to make me more fruitful.
Just as my dad willingly participated in the seasons,
doing what the occasion required, I need to
remember that life, too, has its seasons. If I want
God to be able to reap a harvest through my life,
I need to be willing to let Him prepare the soil—
even if that means experiencing brokenness or pain
or humbling experiences or lessons of waiting.

What about you? Do you sense that you have rocks
that need to be removed before you will be more
receptive to spiritual growth? Have you asked God
to do spring plowing in your life? Have you invited
Him to break up the hard places? I encourage you to

allow Him to do it, even if it feels painful. Take some time to study the "seed and soil" passage from Matthew 13, and think about how God is preparing you to be more receptive for His Word and His will to take root.

 Lord, how often we say that we want You to use us, that we want to be all that we can be for You. And yet we realize that means You will break up the fallow ground in our lives. That process may be painful. But we invite You to do it because we want to be receptive soil in which Your Word and Your will can grow. Give us courage and willingness to be disturbed and corrected and softened. May we gladly stay in "Your program," knowing that You are working all things for our good. Lord, we yield our all to You. Amen.

Sow for yourselves righteousness; reap in mercy;
break up your fallow ground, for it is time to seek the Lord,
till He comes and rains righteousness on you.

HOSEA 10:12

I HAVE BEEN REFLECTING ON THE INESTIMABLE VALUE OF
"BROKEN THINGS." BROKEN PITCHERS GAVE AMPLE LIGHT FOR
VICTORY (JUDGES 7:19-21); BROKEN BREAD WAS MORE THAN
ENOUGH FOR ALL THE HUNGRY (MATTHEW 14:19-21); A
BROKEN BOX GAVE FRAGRANCE TO ALL THE WORLD (MARK
14:3, 9); AND A BROKEN BODY IS SALVATION TO ALL WHO
BELIEVE AND RECEIVE THE SAVIOR (ISAIAH 53:5-6, 12;
1 CORINTHIANS 11:24). AND WHAT CANNOT THE BROKEN
ONE DO WITH OUR BROKEN PLANS, PROJECTS, AND HEART?

V. Raymond Edman, quoted in *Quotable Quotations*

CHAPTER TWENTY

Mountain Climbing

*I*t was not easy to get there, but the memory of it
draws me. I long to revisit that beautiful meadow
that lies near the summit of a rugged mountain not
far from my home.

Friends told Bill and me that the hike was worth
the trek, so several summers ago with three of our
children—Chris, Andy, and Amy—we started out. As
we marched up single file through a tunnel of trees,
the path seemed to go nowhere. It wound up and
around for miles through tall stands of trees. Several
times we found ourselves at a fork in the path, and
we wondered which of the paths that angled out was

the main one. As we trudged upward, we were not always sure that we had stayed on the right course. The path itself was rocky, tedious, and dangerous.

When the kids grumbled about their aching legs or when one of us nearly twisted an ankle, I began to wonder whether the effort was worth it. But then, just when I thought the trip had been a ridiculous waste of a summer Saturday, the fragrance of wildflowers filled the air. *How could this be?* I thought. *It's dark here. The sunlight is screened out by dense trees.* The floor of the forest was quiet and barren beneath the moss hanging from tall fir trees. But soon the path widened, and there it was: a beautiful, sun-drenched meadow fed by streams that cascaded from a glacier clinging to the side of the mountain. We caught our breath. It was too lovely to imagine.

The meadow was a mass of wildflowers of every variety, growing so thickly that the meadow reminded me of an enormous English garden. Enchanted, we took off our shoes and sat by the stream. Surely this must be like heaven, we thought. We ate our lunch, savoring our surroundings. All too soon it was time to go back.

As we made our way down the mountain, I thought of Jesus and His disciples on the Mount of Transfiguration, when God's glory came and Moses and Elijah spoke with Jesus (see Luke 9:28-36). I can identify with Peter, who, after having this glorious mountaintop experience with the Lord, suggested, "Let's build a temple here so that we can come here often and make this experience last forever!"

Like Peter, I would like to "enshrine" the mountaintop experiences, to capture those rare places of victory when I sense God's presence, His pleasure in me. Certain times in my life are like the sun-drenched meadow. I love the times when I feel at one with my husband, and we hold each other, awed at being in love nearly thirty years. Being a mother is wonderful when things are going well with my children. I am positive and excited about following God when I feel I am having success at work and in ministry. I am in a beautiful place, and I want to stay there.

But to be honest, those times are rare. Many more times of my life are like the climb up the mountain—exhausting, uncertain, painful, tedious. Bill and I have had rocky times. Sometimes mothering is very hard work. Some days the ministry God has called me to feels as if it isn't going anywhere.

But the longer I live, the more convinced I am that the struggle—the journey itself—is significant, necessary. For the "joy that was set before Him," Jesus endured the cross (Hebrews 12:2). Endurance is a difficult path, and often it's lonely. And yet struggle is honest and very, very human.

*T*O GET TO THE BEAUTIFUL PLACES, YOU MUST ENDURE.

During a long illness, a friend of mine asked, "Has my life made a difference? Has all of this been worth it?" She, like most of us, wanted her life to count. When the Lord revealed to her that He was using her life—and her struggle—to encourage others, she found the courage to endure the long journey of illness, which recently ended in her death. She persisted because she trusted that the journey had purpose.

Perhaps there is something in your life now that is a struggle for you—even though you know it is right— and you are tempted to give up. Many voices today would tell you that nobody should have to work this hard, that nothing is worth this kind of pain. But the battle is won not so much in blinding moments of truth as it is in hanging in there when the going is tough. Don't give up. If you are following the Lord, the path will lead to a beautiful place. Keep climbing. It is worth the pain.

Remember that there are songs yet to be sung. Paintings yet to be created. Books yet to be written. Lives to be touched for God. Families to be forged. Marriages to be crafted. Lives of integrity yet to be lived. For you to attain these things, you must persevere, staying on the path, allowing God's Word to light your way (see Psalm 119:105).

Just as we experienced on our hike, when the path seemed darkest, we caught the fragrance of wildflowers. I believe that if we open our eyes to God in the midst of our struggles, the fragrance of His presence is with us. And His presence will urge us to stay the course. "Do not throw away this confident trust in the Lord, no matter what happens. Remember the great reward it brings you! Patient endurance is what you need now, so you will continue to do God's will. Then you will receive all that he has promised" (Hebrews 10:35-36, NLT).

Lord, sometimes we get a vision of a lovely ideal that You call us to— something we can do or be. Then we begin the journey, and we find that it is hard. Sometimes it feels too hard and lonely, and we're tempted to give up. Lord, keep before us Your example— that in order to purchase our redemption, You endured the Cross for us. We humbly thank You and rejoice that in our human struggles, You are perfecting us and helping us become real followers of You. In Christ's name, amen.

We can rejoice, too, when we run into problems and trials,
for we know that they are good for us—they help us learn to endure.
And endurance develops strength of character in us,
and character strengthens our confident expectation of salvation.
And this expectation will not disappoint us. For we know how dearly
God loves us, because he has given us the
Holy Spirit to fill our hearts with his love.

ROMANS 5:3-5, NLT

IF WE ARE GOING TO LIVE AS DISCIPLES OF JESUS, WE HAVE
TO REMEMBER THAT ALL NOBLE THINGS ARE DIFFICULT.
THE CHRISTIAN LIFE IS GLORIOUSLY DIFFICULT,
BUT THE DIFFICULTY OF IT DOES NOT MAKE US FAINT
AND CAVE IN; IT ROUSES US UP TO OVERCOME.

Oswald Chambers, *My Utmost for His Highest*

CHAPTER TWENTY-ONE

Harvesttime

*M*other and Dad were in the dining room having coffee and discussing the upcoming harvest. Dad needed to hire extra men, and Mother wondered if she should hire a local girl to help with chores. I—a skinny, blonde, ten-year-old with big ideas—hung around them, absorbing their excitement, longing to be involved. Harvest was everything, the apex of the year, and there was plenty of work to go around. I interrupted, "I can help out in the field. I can drive the truck! I can cook."

Dad looked at me with amusement. "You? You can't drive a truck. You're just a little girl."

Mother saw my disappointment. Defending me, she replied, "She's part of it, Gunder. She can help." I did find my place in the harvest that year. It was in the kitchen, next to Mother.

During harvest, the men would come in at noon for Mother's dinners. Sometimes it was chicken-fried steak with mashed potatoes and gravy, steaming bowls of vegetables, salad, and Mother's famous huckleberry pie for dessert. Always there was plenty of food, with lots of dishes to wash. In the early evening, Mother would send my sisters and me out to the fields to take the men a cold supper so that they could work late into the night. My sisters and I would drive carefully over the bumpy, harvested fields, finding the men by the big red combines that made long shadows against the yellow fields in the late afternoon. Dad and the men were always glad to see us, grateful for the cold drinks we brought in big jugs.

As some of the workers ate, I would watch as the combine poured out the golden grain into the bed of the truck to be hauled to the elevator. I loved every part of it, and I was so glad that my dad allowed me to have a place in the harvest activities.

When I was a teenager, I dreamed of having a

place in the Lord's harvest activities, too. At missionary services in our local church, I would sing with the congregation, "I'll go where you want me to go, dear Lord; o'er mountain, o'er plain, o'er sea. I'll be what you want me to be, dear Lord. . . ." Years later, when I was a young mother, I stood with my husband, Bill, at his ordination service. Shivers went down my spine as we heard the awesome commission: Preach the Word! I accepted the challenge along with Bill, finding my place in the harvest field.

At this season of my life, everything seems to change at a dizzying rate. My life today seems dominated by calendars and commitments, and service to Christ becomes complicated by contracts, budgets, and job descriptions. Once again I pray, "Lord, where is my place in Your harvest field? What do You want me to be doing?"

Yesterday, my daughter, Amy, and I left the supermarket after shopping for groceries, and the early evening traffic was heavy as we waited to enter the highway.

"Mom, look," Amy said softly. A young woman stood next to our car, holding a sign that said, Hungry. Will Work for Food. Amy offered, "Mom, I can give her the box of animal crackers I just bought."

We watched as the woman faced the heavy stream of traffic, an unreadable expression on her young face, maybe of desperate bravado.

WE FIND OUR PLACE IN THE HARVEST
WHEN WE ALLOW GOD TO USE US
RIGHT WHERE WE ARE.

I opened my mouth to tell Amy that this was probably a racket, that the woman most likely earned lots of money from people's guilt as they exited the grocery store. Instead I said lamely, "I guess we could share some of our groceries."

We circled back into the parking lot and fixed up a bag of groceries, with Amy's box of animal crackers on top. We drove back to the woman, and as Amy handed her the bag, the woman began to cry. "God bless you," she said. Amy and I left in tears, too, moved. We simply gave her what we had, yet it somehow felt pivotal, profound.

As we drove home, I thought about the deeper hunger people have—the hunger for the Bread of Life, Jesus. I was quick to assume that afternoon that the woman's "God bless you" indicated that she knew about Jesus, but maybe that wasn't the case.

Sometimes I regret that we didn't take more time to make sure that she had spiritual food as well as a bag of groceries. I'm seeing that the biggest step to being involved in the harvest is simply to be aware that there is one. My life can be so scheduled with activities that I can forget the *lost.*

The lost are all around us—our neighbors, friends, family members. And Jesus always shines the brightest from us when we allow people directly into our lives despite our flaws and simply give out of what He has given us.

It doesn't really matter what job we have in the harvest. What matters is whether or not we are willing to be involved. The Lord of the harvest says, "You are needed in the kingdom. The harvest is great, and the laborers are few."

What is your place in the harvest? Are you willing to see the lost? Are you willing to be His hand extended? Are you willing to allow the Lord to use you?

Remember that God always deals with us where we are, with what we have. It can be intimidating to witness about Jesus. When we are fully in love with Jesus ourselves, it is natural to share Him with others. Remember that it's relationship, not religion, that people need. We only must be willing to share out of what He has given us.

What a great joy to be able to give the Bread of Heaven to a world that so desperately needs Him. Spiritual harvests are preceded by prayer and the sowing of the Word of God. If you are wondering how you can be involved in a more vital way in God's harvest field, begin now to pray, to seek God earnestly. Then wait for Him to show you your place, often using you just where you are.

 Lord, I do not say, "Be with me,"
for, of course, You are! I say, "Open my
eyes to Your Presence." May my spirit
be open to You in a fresh way, and may
I so burn with Your contagious love for
the lost that others are drawn to You.
Help me to see the harvest—wherever
I am—and joyfully accept my place in
it. In Jesus' name, amen.

But when He saw the multitudes, He was moved with compassion for them, because they were weary and scattered, like sheep having no shepherd. Then He said to His disciples, "The harvest truly is plentiful, but the laborers are few. Therefore pray the Lord of the harvest to send out laborers into His harvest."

MATTHEW 9:36-38

UNDERSTANDING WHAT GOD IS ABOUT TO DO WHERE YOU ARE IS MORE IMPORTANT THAN TELLING GOD WHAT YOU WANT TO DO FOR HIM. . . . GOD HASN'T TOLD US TO GO AWAY AND DO SOME WORK FOR HIM. HE HAS TOLD US THAT HE IS ALREADY AT WORK TRYING TO BRING A LOST WORLD TO HIMSELF. IF WE WILL ADJUST OUR LIVES TO HIM IN A LOVE RELATIONSHIP, HE WILL SHOW US WHERE HE IS AT WORK.

Henry Blackaby, *Experiencing God*

CHAPTER TWENTY-TWO

On Receiving Gifts

*C*hristmas 1986 was the first year we had a video camera, and we recorded every gruesome detail, from Christmas Eve through the entire Christmas Day. Nothing was spared.

Andy was eight that Christmas. Loaded up with sugar and adrenaline, he was bouncing off the walls, usually in front of the camera. Bill kept yelling to Andy, "Move!" as *The Nutcracker* ballet played in the background.

Christmas 1986 was the Christmas Bill and I promised each other we would keep spending down. We determined we would be grateful for the little things. We had very good intentions.

But our expectations were not in sync with our intentions. When I opened my present from Bill, I was stunned to see that the gift my dream man had given me was not a soft, blue sweater but a dictionary and a thesaurus, still factory-wrapped in cellophane. You can see on the video my frozen smile and polite, "Fabulous. Just what I need for some writing projects." What you don't see are the tears I shed later in the day as I asked, frustrated, "A dictionary! What do you think I am—a librarian?"

I wasn't alone in my disappointment. Christmas 1986 was the year that I gave Bill a shirt that was too small; he asked if I wished he weighed less. We gave Chris a chemistry set that he never took out of the box. Bill purchased a hefty book on fishing for Jon and one on golf for Eric; neither son was very happy. Only Andy and Amy were happy with their Star Wars stuff and Cabbage Patch things.

Christmas 1986 reminds me of the Christmas when I was ten. I was expecting a fun gift. Instead, I got a manicure set in a little zippered case, a gift my mother thought would be perfect for me. After our family had opened our presents, I heard the phone ring. It was my friend Debbie, wanting to know what I got for Christmas. She always got wonderful gifts.

Her parents were younger than mine, and they had a TV, so they knew what was cool. Debbie's gifts always made mine feel even less adequate.

Most of you have had experiences like these, when you were disappointed with a gift you received because you had expected—and hoped for—something different from what you got. What is it about receiving gifts? Why do we often feel so displeased?

I know I'm supposed to be thankful for gifts I receive, but deep inside I often feel frustrated because I expected something fantastic and marvelous. And then I fall into the trap of comparing my gift with what other people got, and that only makes me feel even more disappointed.

I learned some sobering, but freeing, lessons about expectations and gratitude in a most unlikely place—through the adoption of our daughter.

After Bill and I had been blessed with four sons, we longed for a daughter. We prayed about that, and God led us to adopt Amy.

Our Amy came off the plane into our arms and hearts from a Korean orphanage when she was three years old. I had definite ideas about what my daughter would be like. I tried sharing my love of books with Amy, but learning disabilities made reading hard for her. I enrolled her in ballet, but she was miserable. I signed her up for piano lessons, but she wanted to play basketball. I bought her adorable dresses and ribbons, but she preferred jeans and high-top tennis shoes. She loved animals, but I sneeze around anything on four legs.

*S*OMETIMES THE VERY BEST GIFTS
WE RECEIVE ARE NOT THE
ONES WE WANTED.

A level of frustration and anger toward Amy began to simmer inside me. Amy was angry at me, too, and was obstinate and difficult to manage at times. One day she blew up at me. "I hate you! I wish you weren't my mother. Why did you adopt me? I don't want to be in this family!" Her angry outburst shocked me. For a day she was stormy, refusing to talk to me.

"God," I prayed, "what am I doing to this child?" I was ashamed to admit my gut-level emotions: This gift was not what I'd expected, not what I'd wanted.

In His still, small voice, God said, "Some of the very best gifts I give you are not the ones you wanted. Love her for who she is, not for what you want her to be for you. Don't compare her to some ideal. Accept her for the beautiful gift that she is."

That was one of the defining moments of my life, and I determined to thank God for the gift of Amy. As I learned to appreciate her for who she is, I began to see a beautiful, sturdy little soul with a heart of compassion and unique talents. But I had to back off and study her—to see her for who she is, not for what I wanted her to be.

Amy has taught me much about real love and success. What changed? Me, not Amy. Amy was the same wonderful person all along. I just had to see her, to thank God for her.

You, too, have been given precious, unique gifts— that of heritage, family, and individual talents. But perhaps God has given you a gift that you haven't thanked Him for yet. You may see this "gift" as a burden.

I encourage you to confess your disappointment to God and to ask Him to help you to be grateful. It will amaze you how thanking God for His gifts—even the ones you didn't want—will change your attitude and help you see how wonderful they really are.

Oh, the dictionary and the thesaurus? I probably

use them far more than any other gift my husband has given me—which reminds me that God knows exactly what we need in our lives. We must learn to receive His gifts with thanks, knowing they are true blessings from Him.

 Lord, thank You for daily loading us with benefits! Your goodness is overwhelming. Forgive us for wanting what we don't have and for not wanting what we do have. Some things are easier to thank You for than others— especially the gifts that puzzle and burden us. But as we place our lives in Your hands, we realize that You indeed are in control and that as a loving Father, You have our good in mind. So we thank You for what You have given us. Make us good stewards of Your gifts, Lord, that our lives would overflow with praise and thanksgiving. In Jesus' name, amen.

Every good gift and every perfect gift is from above,
and comes down from the Father of lights,
with whom there is no variation or shadow of turning.

JAMES 1:17

SO MANY ARE GOD'S KINDNESSES TO US, THAT,

AS DROPS OF WATER, THEY RUN TOGETHER;

AND IT IS NOT UNTIL WE ARE BORNE UP BY THE MULTITUDE

OF THEM, AS BY STREAMS IN DEEP CHANNELS,

THAT WE RECOGNIZE THEM AS COMING FROM HIM.

WE HAVE WALKED AMID HIS MERCIES AS IN A FOREST WHERE

WE ARE TANGLED AMONG TEN THOUSAND GROWTHS AND

TOUCHED ON EVERY HAND BY LEAVES AND BUDS WHICH

WE NOTICE NOT. WE CANNOT RECALL ALL THE THINGS

HE HAS DONE FOR US. THEY ARE SO MANY.

Henry Ward Beecher, quoted in *Treasury of the Christian Faith*

CHAPTER TWENTY-THREE

The Reluctant Pioneer

I recently discovered that the old Santiam Wagon Road goes right by our house. While some of the road still cuts an unmistakable swath through the giant Ponderosa pines as it winds its way west toward Oregon's Santiam Pass over the Cascades, other parts of the trail are now overgrown by smaller trees and interrupted by logging roads.

It's amazing to think that a little more than a hundred years ago, wagons tediously pushed their way through this region on their way to the fertile Willamette Valley. Most of the pioneers went along the more-defined Oregon Trail, but a few came this way looking for a better route to the promised land.

Intrigued by the people who trudged these trails, I went to the library, eager to check out books and learn about the pioneers' experiences. Many of the books I found were old, barely used, and long out of print. One book, *The Reluctant Pioneer,* caught my eye. It's the story of Mary Adams, mother of six, who with her family and several other members of their Methodist church left Iowa in 1852 in the rush to settle Oregon. Like many women pioneers, she had not wanted to leave her home. Part of her reluctance was because she was pregnant. But Mary's husband persuaded her that it was their patriotic duty to win Oregon for the United States, and he promised that he would get her there safely. The trip turned out to be horrendous, with many in their party dying of cholera on the way. Although Mary's husband did get her to Oregon, she became very ill after the birth of her baby, and she died shortly after she got there.

Another diary records that when a wagon train reached the Great Basin of Utah and Nevada, one woman was overcome by the thought of the rest of the journey and refused to go another step. Knowing that the rest of the travelers were impatient to move on, her husband finally said, "Then I'll just leave you here."

"Fine!" was her reply, so he left. When he turned around to look at her one more time, he saw that she had set fire to the wagon. He went back at a gallop, put her on his horse, and hauled her kicking and screaming back to the rest of the wagon train. Now that was a reluctant pioneer.

My imagination runs wild as I think about those pioneer women. How surprised they would be to travel the Santiam Wagon Road today and see pavement and houses. Their journey west was painstakingly slow as they carved out new roads, averaging about ten miles a day—a distance I travel in fifteen minutes when I take Amy to school. The pioneers dealt with Indian hostilities, buffalo stampedes, cholera, childbirth on the trail, and disease. Their biggest enemies were hunger, lack of water, and extreme weather. Many couldn't take the rigors of the trail and went back east to the more established territories. But their personal diaries show that despite the hardship and their initial reluctance, many knew that they were part of a difficult but exhilarating event. They were willing to suffer inconvenience and risk failure because they felt the strong need to face the challenge.

When I walk along that old path today, I look at the worn tracks with new appreciation. I am inspired by these pioneers. I wonder if I would have had the courage to press on. I look at my own life and ask, What areas need that same kind of pioneering faith? What worlds are left to conquer?

CONQUERING NEW TERRITORY DEMANDS HAVING COURAGE AND LEAVING OUR COMFORT ZONE.

The earth seems weary, groaning for its redemption. The most challenging quest of all, I believe, is to share Jesus in these spiritually perilous times. To me, to be a pioneer for God means to say yes to opportunities to share Christ in fresh ways so that people will listen and understand—a task that seems daunting, yet inexplicably thrilling.

I do tend to be a reluctant pioneer. I could be content to have a cabin by the side of the road and listen to others' stories of faith, not make my own. Following God is fine as long as I'm comfortable. But He says, "There's territory to claim if you dare to follow Me."

Different times call for different kinds of faith. There's a pioneering faith, and there's a settler's faith, and God needs both. Esther in the Old Testament had a pioneering faith when she went before the king, literally putting her life on the line to save her people. Her uncle said, "Who knows whether you have come to the kingdom for such a time as this?" (Esther 4:14).

Perhaps God is calling you to greater challenges of faith, and you are wondering whether to risk security for obedience. It's true that following Christ often means leaving our comfort zones and moving into the unknown. Yet following Him results in the greatest security ever because He never abandons us or leads us astray.

As we walk the worn path of others who followed Jesus at great personal price, it's good to stop and ask some questions: Who will be following our footsteps? Will they see that we were reluctant pioneers? Or will they see that we established new territory for God? The cloud of witnesses cheers us on: "Stay the course. Keep the faith! Fight the good fight! There is a crown to be won, victory to be had."

Lord, thank You for reminding us that You have so much more for us if we will just have the courage to follow You. Forgive us for wanting to be safe and comfortable and complacent. Thank You for reminding us that we don't need to have everything all spelled out, that it's enough to follow You. Help us to trust that You know the way. May we diligently study Your Word and have the courage to engage the opportunities You place in our path. In Jesus' name we pray, amen.

By faith Abraham obeyed when he was called to go out to the place
which he would receive as an inheritance. And he went out,
not knowing where he was going. By faith he dwelt in the land of
promise as in a foreign country, dwelling in tents with Isaac and
Jacob, the heirs with him of the same promise; for he waited for
the city which has foundations, whose builder and maker is God.

HEBREWS 11:8-10

THERE IS A FIRST FAITH AND A SECOND FAITH. THE FIRST
FAITH IS THE EASY, TRADITIONAL BELIEF OF CHILDHOOD,
TAKEN FROM OTHER PEOPLE, BELIEVED BECAUSE IT BELONGS
TO THE TIME AND LAND. THE SECOND FAITH IS THE PERSONAL
CONVICTION OF THE SOUL. IT IS THE HEART KNOWING,
BECAUSE GOD HAS SPOKEN TO IT.

Phillips Brooks, *Treasury of the Christian Faith*

CHAPTER TWENTY-FOUR

Best Friends

When our son Eric was three, he was the middle child. Jon was a couple of years older, and Chris was the baby. We had recently moved, leaving behind all that was familiar to Eric—except Charlie Beakey, Eric's imaginary friend, who stuck with him through thick and thin. Charlie was an ideal friend: He never argued; he played whatever Eric wanted to play; and he was always there for Eric. After a year or two, though, Eric replaced Charlie Beakey with real friends.

Unfortunately, real people aren't perfect. This week, Amy, now a freshman in high school, and I had a long discussion about her current friendships, which seem quite complicated. I was tempted to tell her, "Oh, get over it!" when I remembered my own early teen years. I had a best friend through child-hood. We took turns spending the night at each other's houses and shared secrets. We pledged our undying loyalty and promised to be in each other's weddings. But when we reached high school, things changed. Our interests took us in different direc-tions, and we made new friends. For some time I had a sense of loss over the change in our best-friend status, and although we said hello to each other in the hallway, we were never best friends again.

My friends are precious to me. I *need* them, and I want to take good care of my friendships, even though there have been times when I haven't been there for my friends as I should have been. (I've been known to be so late with birthday cards that the recipient thought I was early.) But my friends are forgiving and faithful, and I am humbly grateful.

After all, there is only one perfect Friend. John 13 through 17 gives an amazing description of Jesus and His disciples during the Passover meal in the upper room, just before the Crucifixion. What a ragtag bunch Jesus' disciples were! And yet He spent three years eating and sleeping with them and pouring His life into them. The Passover scene is especially poignant. "You are My friends," He told them, as He washed their feet, prayed for them, and broke bread with them.

Judas, who betrayed the Lord for thirty pieces of silver, was also part of the group. Of course, I would expect bad things from Judas. But the rest of the disciples—how could they have been so unfaithful? In the Garden of Gethsemane, Jesus asked them to watch and pray. But in the hours of Jesus' greatest agony, while He wrestled with the realities of the cup His Father had for Him, His friends didn't come through. "Could you not watch one hour?" Jesus asked them (Mark 14:37).

I can understand the disciples' fear. They didn't want to get the same treatment Jesus got, and that certainly seemed a real possibility, with the presence of the Roman soldiers and the ugly mood of the crowd. How was it, though, that these men who had followed Jesus night and day and had pledged their undying loyalty could go from discussing lofty eternal truths to falling apart when He needed them the most? To not even be able to stay awake and pray?

I like to think I would have been there for Jesus. That I wouldn't have panicked. That I wouldn't have been petty. That I would have prayed with Him in His great agony, even if I didn't understand what was going on. But I'm afraid I'm one of the ragtag bunch myself. I can sit around and discuss spiritual things, pretend to have it all together; then, when my back is against the wall, I'm thinking of my own skin. Intercessory prayer? I try. But intercession is not very glamorous. I can get serious about prayer when it's *my* needs I'm praying for. But if it's for the body of Christ at large or someone I don't know very well, I am not so moved to pray. Fasting is hard for me. And if someone's need to be served inconveniences me, I can get evasive, busy with other things. Like the disciples, my intentions are good, but I'm not always there for Jesus.

WE HONOR JESUS BY BEING A FRIEND TO THOSE HE PLACES IN OUR LIVES.

Jesus never fails *us,* though. Never. He loves us where we are, but He also sees what we can be. He is the best Friend anyone could have, and He is real, not a figment of our imagination. The friendship Jesus offers is not one to take lightly. It cost Him His very life. It is a holy, exclusive relationship, a best-friend relationship. And the more we know Him, the more we can honor Him by being a friend to those He places in our lives.

Do you need a friend? Try this: Be the kind of friend to someone else that you yourself would like to have. True friendship takes time—it takes opening up, allowing others into our lives and sharing in theirs, and going the extra mile with a person who needs someone to help carry the load. Jesus sacrificed His very life to be our Friend. If we are to know true friendship with others, we must follow Jesus' example of sacrifice. It's not easy, but the rewards are well worth it.

Lord, You created us with a capacity for friendship, and how we need it in life's ebbs and flows. May we learn from Your example how to be a real friend: to be inconvenienced, to care about what our friend is going through, to be there for her. Life can be lonely and hard. Thank You for being a best friend to us by giving Your very life—the greatest test of friendship ever. And, Lord, may I show by my life that I want to be Your friend, too. Amen.

[Jesus said,] "I have called you friends."

JOHN 15:15

JESUS! WHAT A FRIEND FOR SINNERS!
JESUS! LOVER OF MY SOUL;

FRIENDS MAY FAIL ME, FOES ASSAIL ME,
HE, MY SAVIOR MAKES ME WHOLE.

HALLELUJAH! WHAT A SAVIOR! HALLEUJAH! WHAT A FRIEND!

SAVING, HELPING, KEEPING, LOVING,
HE IS WITH ME TO THE END.

J. Wilbur Chapman, "Jesus! What a Friend for Sinners!"

CHAPTER TWENTY-FIVE

The Life God Uses

*I*t was 1967, and Bill and I were newly married. Besides being a youth pastor, Bill was in graduate school. I worked full-time, helping him the best I could. Life was busy. One evening at a gathering with several other couples, the leader of the group turned to me and said, "Nancie, why don't you share with us what God is doing in your life?" I gulped, my face turning red. I hated the word *share;* it seemed so overused. Besides, it didn't seem to me that God was doing anything in my life. But I knew the Christian lingo, so I managed to rattle off something phony. Later the question burned inside of me: *How do you get something to share?*

Lately I've been considering what it means to really "share" from my life. Maybe it's because I'm turning the big "five-oh" the end of this year. Or maybe it's because very soon, I'll be a grandmother for the first time. But somehow it seems urgent that I give God full permission to use me any way He will. I believe He's calling me to be a leader, to share (there's that word again) from my life. A leader is anyone with influence, so actually all of us are leaders of some kind.

When I was a senior in high school, a local service group gave me a scholarship for exemplifying leadership. At one of the group's meetings I gave a short speech but felt like an impostor. *Me—a leader?* I privately scoffed. I'm not a natural organizer, and I struggled with the idea of being in front of a group. I still do. But I can't get away from the fact that God has given me so much. So how can I *not* share? I am learning these important principles about letting God use my life:

I must be willing. When God called Moses to leave the land of Midian and go back to lead His people out of Egypt, Moses didn't have confidence in his own abilities. He begged God to use someone else. But he began to tentatively follow God, and over time God made him a great leader. Before the prophet Isaiah could share God's truth, he had to come to a place of humility and submission: Then he said to God, "Here am I. Send me."

I must have faith in something bigger than I am. Moses was able to carry out his task because he got his directive from God. He kept his eye on the big picture. Earlier, when Moses intervened in a fight between two Israelite slaves, they did not welcome his input with open arms. "Who made you a ruler over us?" they demanded. If people responded to me the way the Israelites did to Moses, I would burst into tears and resign! But Moses kept listening to God. What holds me is belief in God's Son, Jesus Christ, and in the fact that the Bible is God's Word, relevant for today.

I must seek out mentors. Moses gained knowledge growing up in the Egyptian court, and practical wisdom from his father-in-law, Jethro. Seeking out mentors for different times and challenges in my life is an ongoing process. Quiet time with God and His Word mentors me. God has put my parents, my husband, and many special people into my life.

Thought-provoking books by ancient and contemporary authors influence me. And now I find myself being mentored in surprising ways by my growing-up children.

GOD TESTS AND PURIFIES HIS MESSAGE IN THE LIVES OF THOSE HE USES.

I must not allow failure to keep me from sharing. Passionate commitment to something bigger than I am helps me to not be defeated by my own inevitable mistakes. Failures can be embarrassing, humiliating, hard on my pride. But with God's forgiveness and mercy, I can go on so that those failures are not what defines my life. It is amazing to think God can use me, mistakes and all. As I look back at the few times when I think God really used me, I am humbled to see that it was in spite of myself. True sharing comes out of what God has given us.

Disappointments don't eliminate the message; they only refine it. Recently, after a disappointment related to sharing, I said, "Never again! Forget speaking; forget being a leader. What do I have to say, anyway? Let somebody else do it, someone who can do it better." It's true that someone else *could* do it—God's work doesn't hinge on me. But *I* would be missing out. And God uses disappointments to help refine His message in my life.

Ask yourself: Am I willing for God to use me where I am? What do I have to share with others out of the difficulties I've experienced? Remember, God tests and purifies His message in the lives of the people He chooses to use. And it is in the testing, the painful trials, that God makes Himself real to us. When you allow God's grace fully into your disappointments and failures, He will give you an honest and strong message that you can share with others.

Lord, You have given us so much. We are like clay in Your hands. Continue to mold and shape us into Your image, so that even the painful experiences become monuments to Your mighty provision. I pray that we will be generous people, giving people, who are willing to share with others from the abundance of what You have brought into our lives. And as we do, may others be drawn to You. In Jesus' name, amen.

Then I heard the Lord asking, "Whom should I send as
a messenger to my people? Who will go for us?"
And I said, "Lord, I'll go! Send me."
ISAIAH 6:8, NLT

THE ONE WHO HAS HAD BUT LITTLE TROUBLE IN LIFE IS NOT
A PARTICULARLY HELPFUL PERSON. BUT ONE WHO HAS GONE
THROUGH A HUNDRED AND ONE TRIALS, EXPERIENCES,
DEATHS, BLASTED HOPES, SHOCKS, AND A TRAGEDY OR TWO
AND HAS LEARNED HIS LESSON . . . SUCH A PERSON IS
WORTHWHILE. HE IS ABLE TO ENTER INTO THE NEED OF
SUFFERING HUMANITY AND PRAY IT THROUGH. HE CAN ENTER
INTO PERFECT FELLOWSHIP WITH A PERSON WHO IS IN
UNSPOKEN AGONY OF SPIRIT AND PRESSURE OF TRIAL.
HE IS ABLE TO LOOK BEYOND THE FRAILTY OF FLESH AND,
REMEMBERING WE ARE BUT DUST, TO TRUST GOD WITH A
SUBLIME FAITH FOR VICTORY AND POWER. DO NOT BE AFRAID
OF THE PROCESS. I SEE SUCH RICH POSSIBILITIES IN IT ALL.
WE LONG TO BE OF SERVICE TO NEEDY MANKIND.
NOTHING CAN BETTER EQUIP US THAN TO BREAK IN SPIRIT
AND HEART AND SO BECOME CLEAR, SPARKLING WINE,
RICH AND REFRESHING.

J. W. Follette, *Broken Bread*

179

CHAPTER TWENTY-SIX

Trees of Righteousness

I sit with my morning coffee, looking out onto a frosty scene. Most mornings the sun fills this room, but this morning a fine, steady snow is falling, and it's so cold that the snow seems to have to force its way down. This is a real January snow, not a December Christmas-card one.

Directly outside my dining-room window stands a magnificent ponderosa pine tree that we've been told is two hundred or more years old. It has seen a lot under the central Oregon sky: forest fires; blustery springs; hot, dry summers; freezing winters. It was likely a mute witness as Native Americans hunted deer, elk, and bear. Now it has the Carmichael family snuggled up next to it. And still it stands, impervious to all around it—lifting its elegant branches toward heaven.

I haven't seen as many seasons as our tree (although my daughter thinks I have), yet I am affected by their passing. Now I am feeling keenly the effects of an emptying nest. I have experienced other seasons, too, that may be less obvious but are just as real. I went through a season of *idealism* in my youth, when I lived mainly on hopes and dreams and nothing seemed impossible. Then I went through a season of *invincibility*, when I was convinced that if I followed a certain formula, I would succeed. Those early seasons were sunny, warm times when the world seemed right side up. Midlife seems to have its share of storms, often unpredictable and scary. The other day I listened to a friend who is having a crisis in her family, and I was reminded again that it rains on the just and on the unjust. Sometimes things happen with no apparent explanation. She'd done everything "right," yet she is now in desperate need of God's intervention.

I have also experienced seasons of *blessing*, when I've sensed God's presence so strongly it was almost tangible. Times when God has answered my prayers in a special way and I see Him moving in our family, our church, all around us. I like this rare season best, and I tend to think, *Finally! This is the way it should always be!* But it's not always that way.

Now I find myself in a season of *not knowing.* This is a most difficult place because I like to have loose ends tied up, and the editor in me wants a finished manuscript. But this is where I am learning important lessons about trust. Emerson wrote: "All I have seen teaches me to trust the Creator for all I have not seen." God's very nature is faithfulness, and He cannot deny Himself. Having to trust Him in a season of *not knowing* is an opportunity for my roots to go down deep to find nourishment from His Word, which is faithful and true.

> *B*EING ROOTED AND PLANTED DEEP IN
> GOD WILL BRING STABILITY AND
> LONG-LASTING FRUIT.

What is His message to me in a season of uncertainty? Simply that I must not cast away my confidence. I must listen to the still, small voice that says, *Trust Me. Put aside your striving, your manipulating, and simply trust Me.* It can be hard to listen to that voice when what I *see*

is not faith-inspiring but fear-producing. These are perilous times for people of faith. Fellow believers in some parts of the world are facing persecution, even death, and we must pray for them, stand with them. Even our own culture is subtly, pervasively hostile to righteousness. If I trust what I see, I can become terrified for my children and grandchildren because the lure of the world is so strong, its messages so persistent. But Scripture says that God is able to keep that which I commit to Him. And I do commit them to Him, believing for the best.

Somehow my father, trees, and Psalm 1 are all tied together in my mind because Dad, a righteous man, was *planted* in God. As I sat and studied the ponderosa pine, the words of that psalm came to me:

> Blessed is the man who walks not in the counsel of the ungodly, nor stands in the path of sinners, nor sits in the seat of the scornful; but his delight is in the law of the Lord, and in His law he meditates day and night. He shall be like a tree planted by the rivers of water, that brings forth its fruit in its season, whose leaf also shall not wither; and whatever he does shall prosper. (Psalm 1:1-3)

Shortly after my father died, Mother gave me a black-and-white snapshot of Dad holding me when I was two years old. I cherish that picture because there is something infinitely precious about being held by one's father.

Being rooted and planted in God is like being held by Him. It provides the stability to survive difficult seasons and storms. As I look to the future, I have no idea what's ahead. For now, I am learning to trust. To be deeply rooted in God means we cling to Him when we think we understand—and especially when we don't—knowing that He holds us and all that we commit to Him.

What kind of season are you in now? How are you responding to God there? Your response to Him is what can make you grow deep. It's not the circumstance so much as it is our response to it that makes the difference in the life of one whose trust is in the Lord. Don't give up, and don't be swayed by the negative things you see around you. It is possible for you to be planted in God and have a life that bears fruit. But it takes patience, persistence, and a lot of trusting in the character of God through all seasons of life.

Oh, God, as we change and grow, help us to grow toward You. Keep us from envying those who are planted elsewhere or may be in a season that is different from where we find ourself. Only let us be faithful where You have us. May we put our roots down deep so that we will not be swayed or moved by what we see. Thank You for faithfully holding us. Great is Your faithfulness through all the seasons of life! Amen.

The righteous shall flourish like a palm tree, he shall grow like a cedar in Lebanon. Those who are planted in the house of the Lord shall flourish in the courts of our God. They shall still bear fruit in old age; they shall be fresh and flourishing.

PSALM 92:12-14

REAL TRUST DOESN'T OCCUR UNTIL WE'VE COMMITTED
THE FULL WEIGHT OF OUR HOPES, DREAMS, AND EXPECTATIONS—
OUR VERY LIVES—INTO HIS HANDS.

Ron Mehl, *The Cure for a Troubled Heart*

CHAPTER TWENTY-SEVEN

A Story for My Heart

*W*e called him Teacher, the man who taught me and a dozen others (half of whom were my siblings) in the one-room school in Montana. When it was time for my grade's lesson, Mr. Schwoch would announce, "Fourth grade!" (or whatever grade I was in) and Jimmy Myers, my only other classmate for eight years, and I would walk to the front with our books for our turn with Teacher.

As I learned to enjoy reading on my own, the wonderful world of books opened to me. One day at school I was reading "Reynard the Fox." The story gripped my imagination, and I became enthralled by the vivid characters. To this day I am haunted by the story's theme of friendship, cruelty, and betrayal.

When I finished reading, I took a deep breath and looked up. Everyone was looking at me, and the students were laughing. I had not heard Teacher call my grade, and he and Jimmy had already gone over our lesson while I, oblivious, had been with Reynard. Teacher held up his hand to defend me against the snickers of the other children. "No, no. That's very good. Any time you are captured by a story, I will never disturb you." He was a wise teacher, who didn't let education get in the way of learning. He knew that true learning takes place in an interested, listening heart.

The best stories are those that resonate deep within us. Underlying the obvious plot is another layer, a deeper meaning that echoes through time. I like to poke around old bookstores and look for some of the stories I read and loved as a child: books such as *How Green Was My Valley* and *Shantytown*. These stories generated real emotions. They reminded me that the human experience is common and that what is most personal is also most universal.

Jesus' disciples had been following Him around for a while and had watched Him teach the people by telling them parables. Perhaps storytelling seemed frivolous to them when discussing such weighty matters as the kingdom. His disciples asked Him, "Why do You always tell stories when You talk to the people?"

Jesus said,

> Because people see what I do, but they don't really see. They hear what I say, but they don't really hear, and they don't understand. . . . "The hearts of these people are hardened, and their ears cannot hear, and they have closed their eyes—so their eyes cannot see, and their ears cannot hear, and their hearts cannot understand, and they cannot turn to me and let me heal them." (Matthew 13:13-15, NLT)

Jesus knew that the stories that change us are the ones that make us think and feel, that get past our defenses and get to the real issues. Walter Brueggeman wrote in *Finally Comes the Poet:* "We are not changed by new rules. The deep places in our lives—places of resistance and embrace—are not ultimately reached by instruction. Those places of resistance and embrace are reached only by stories, by images, metaphors and phrases that line out the world differently." When a person's heart is hard, it is difficult for the gospel to penetrate. Sometimes we can be reached by stories—but we must hear the right story.

THERE ARE MANY STORIES THESE DAYS—
BUT FOR GOD TO CHANGE ME,
I MUST HEAR HIS STORY.

Too many distractions—conversation, news, noise, TV, movies—can drown out Jesus' story in our lives. Individually, these things may be harmless; indeed, some may even be stimulating and informative. But when they are constant and overwhelming, they get in the way of the real story that can heal us. Jesus related it to the weeds and thistles that choke out the good seed. This is why it is so essential to saturate our minds with the discipline of reading the Bible with an open heart and pondering what we've read.

Physical distractions aren't the only things that can keep Jesus' story from getting through to us. Unresolved guilt can cause us to become defensive. Stubborn self-righteousness can harden our hearts.

Fear can keep the vibrant truth of the gospel from penetrating to the core of our lives. Our hearts can grow hardened to Jesus' story when we hold on to anger and unforgiveness.

The wonderful thing is that even with our hardened hearts, Jesus loves us. And He spent His life telling stories to reach us, because until His story gets to our hearts, we don't *really* hear, *really* change. We truly hear His story when we identify with it—when we see our own need and His grace that meets our need. Jesus' story forces us to choose. There is no neutral ground with Him. We either respond to His story or, like the rich young ruler, turn away. Responding to Him brings healing; resisting Him hardens our hearts even more. He longs for us to turn to Him and be healed.

There is a very real difference between a hard heart and one that is softened toward the things of God. It is one thing for a teacher to try to cram facts into the head of an unwilling student; it's quite another to teach a student who is *hungry* to know, who *wants* to hear. We must pray for a softened, hungry heart that makes us want to sit at Jesus' feet and listen to His story. Many spellbinding "stories" vie for our attention, but the only thing that will really change us is to be captivated wholeheartedly by Jesus' story and experience the healing and redemption that come as a result.

Lord, how often we are drawn away from the very story that we need to hear—Yours. We are distracted and pulled away, and our eyes and ears get filled with meaningless, trivial stories. Give us a deep hunger and longing to know You, to see ourselves and our great need in Your wonderful story, and to turn to You and be healed. Father, we do present ourselves to You and ask that You would open our eyes and our ears, that we may truly see and hear what You would say to us. In Jesus' name, amen.

Create in me a clean heart, O God, and renew a steadfast spirit within me. . . . The sacrifices of God are a broken spirit, a broken and contrite heart—these O God, You will not despise.

PSALM 51:10, 17

HOW ELSE BUT THROUGH A BROKEN HEART

MAY LORD CHRIST ENTER IN?

Oscar Wilde, *The Ballad of Reading Gaol*

CHAPTER TWENTY-EIGHT

Food from My Garden

Although for now I must be content with hanging baskets that can survive our transient schedule and short growing season, each year in the gentle warmth of spring I have a fleeting desire to have a garden. I have such good memories of my grandmother's garden on our farm in Montana. Every weekend in the spring, my grandmother came out to the farm, and early on Saturday morning, she awakened us children with the promise of pancakes in order to enlist our help with her garden. Dressed in Dad's bib overalls (I never dreamed then that her fashion sense was forty years ahead of time), she would lead us out to weed and water. We knew how good the corn on the cob and string beans would taste later in the summer.

Perhaps someday we will live where I can have a garden and grow wonderful produce for the family. When everyone in our family is home, I need a full refrigerator and pantry. I always know when Andy is home from college because the cereal boxes get emptied. But often it's just Bill and Amy and me, and we don't need much. "How long has this been in here?" Bill asks as he scrutinizes the expiration date on a cereal box.

Cleaning out my refrigerator, freezer, and pantry can feel like an archaeological dig in which the layers tell tales of events and the passing of time. When we lived in the Willamette Valley and fruit was abundant, I canned everything I could get my hands on. The other day, on the top shelf, way in the back, I found a jar of plums from that era. They were so old there wasn't even an expiration date, so I threw them out and saved the jar. We all agree on one thing—we want *fresh*. Fresh, tasty, nutritious food that is good for the body.

At a speaking engagement in California, I met a young woman just out of college. An aspiring writer, she was frustrated at not getting published. I read some of her writing and tried to give her suggestions. I empathized with her, remembering how hard I worked at writing when I was her age, with little reward. Every time I sent an article to a publisher I prayed for acceptance, but often the manuscript came back. My burning desire was to connect with people, to communicate truth. I wanted to feed people with my words, my stories, but I didn't understand that my message wasn't fully developed yet. It has taken me years to see that my life is my real work, my real garden. And like a fruitful garden, I must go through seasons—preparing the soil, planting the seed, watering, weeding, and waiting—before I can produce something that will feed people.

We nurturers all long to feed people, to encourage and love them with real truth. But how do we do that? How do we provide something fresh, nourishing, and life giving that will point people to Christ? When I was very small, I heard a preacher pray before he spoke, "Hide Thy servant behind the Cross." I peeked at him, wondering how he could hide behind the cross, because the cross in the front of the church was very skinny and nailed to the wall.

As WE STAY "IN THE VINE" THROUGH THE SEASONS OF LIFE, WE WILL PRODUCE FRUIT THAT IS NOURISHING, RELEVANT, AND LIFE-GIVING TO OTHERS.

After Jesus' death and resurrection, He taught Peter and several other disciples a lesson about true ministry. They had decided to go fishing but had not caught any fish. After the disciples (except John) had abandoned Jesus in His hour of greatest need, no one would have blamed Jesus for scolding His disciples. But instead, He helped them bring in a huge catch and then cooked fish for their breakfast by the sea.

There is an intriguing interchange between Jesus and Peter. Three times Jesus asked Peter, "Peter, do you love Me?" Each time, Peter answered Him, "Yes, Lord, You know that I love You." And Jesus told him, "Feed My lambs. . . . Tend My sheep. . . . Feed My sheep" (see John chapter 21).

I wonder a lot about this passage. What does it take to truly follow Jesus, to "feed" others out of what He is doing in my life? There are times when I think that I am finished, that I have no more to say, and I'm tempted to just go fishing. But Jesus asks gently, "Do you love Me? Then feed My sheep."

A friend of mine is enduring unbelievable testing. God has used her greatly in the past, but now she is in a time of confusion and pain. As I watch her in this crucible, I truly believe that out of this season will come new growth and insights with which she will again nourish people in a powerful, fresh way. She is literally being hidden by a cross of suffering, but as she stays in Him, there will be fruit from this season. I believe that because her heart is open to God, even now, when she hasn't any answers.

So many of us desperately need to be fed from God, asking inwardly, as Walter Brueggeman put it in *Finally Comes the Poet:* "Is there a word from the Lord that will help me live? Is there a word to rescue me from my exhausted coping?" The answer is, yes, there is, and the word is this: God loves us! That is a magnificent truth, and in order for it to be palatable to others as we share it from our lives, it must not be stale. We must be living and experiencing it now.

Fruit develops in us as we stay "in the vine," go through seasons with Him, invite His presence deep into our lives, be honest about what's there. If we do not gain nourishment from Him, we cannot feed others. It is when He feeds our hearts that we have something to give others—something real, fresh, and nourishing.

 Lord, it isn't enough to give out of stale experiences, out of long past victories and successes. We confess our need and our utter dependence on You to do a fresh work of grace in our lives. May we be up to date in our experience with You, in touch with what You are doing in our lives now, so that what we give to others is real and palatable. In Jesus' name, amen.

Jesus said to Simon Peter, "Simon, son of Jonah, do you love
Me more than these?" He said to Him, "Yes, Lord;
you know that I love You." He said to him, "Feed My lambs."

JOHN 21:15

THE PEOPLE WHO ARE OF ABSOLUTELY NO USE TO GOD ARE
THOSE WHO HAVE SAT DOWN AND HAVE BECOME OVERGROWN
WITH SPIRITUAL MILDEW; ALL THEY CAN DO IS TO REFER TO AN
EXPERIENCE THEY HAD TWENTY OR THIRTY YEARS AGO.
THAT IS OF NO USE WHATEVER; WE MUST BE VITALLY AT IT
ALL THE TIME. WITH PAUL IT WAS NEVER "AN EXPERIENCE
I ONCE HAD," BUT *THE LIFE WHICH I NOW LIVE."*

Oswald Chambers, *Oswald Chambers, The Best from All His Books*

CHAPTER TWENTY-NINE

Preparing the Message

*I*t had been "one of those weeks," full of interruptions and incessant demands. In the back of my mind was the weight of a spiritual retreat I was to lead, beginning on Friday evening, and I was not ready. I had an outline to speak from, but I needed a few solid hours to think and pray. Wednesday arrived, and with it another interruption, as we needed unexpected work done on our house. For two very long days, four workers were my constant companions, as they tried to make our house more energy efficient. *I think* I'm *the one who needs to be more energy efficient,* I thought grimly, wondering how I was going to find time to prepare for the retreat. Friday morning I had an idea: I would leave home early and stop to see our son Andy. The retreat center was close to his college, and after we had lunch together, I would have at least two prime hours of quiet.

I picked Andy up at his apartment and moved over to let him drive. "You choose the place, and I'll buy, Andy."

"Let's see. . . ." He began to drive downtown. "There's a place I think you'd really like." *We're going downtown? I thought. Kind of out of our way. Today would be the day when he isn't in a hurry and I am!* Normally Andy is in a rush to get to a class or to basketball practice, and I'm doing well just to grab a hug from him.

We found the restaurant, ordered, and began catching up on school and news from friends and relatives. Then Andy asked, "What are you going to speak about at the retreat?" I started to answer flippantly; then I saw he really wanted to know, so I told him, "Well, tonight I'm going to talk about the gift of life that each of us has—how precious it is."

"That's cool. Say, Mom, aren't we close to the cemetery where Aunt Char and Uncle Bob's baby was buried?" He began asking questions about the little cousin he never knew, how her life had been cut short at three months, and how her death had affected the family. As we left the restaurant, Andy suggested, "Let's go visit the cemetery." The day was sunny and sweet, and the beautiful colors of the trees and shrubs that are so plentiful in the Willamette Valley beckoned us outside.

We turned off a busy street onto a quiet side road and found the cemetery. It had been many years since I was there, and we walked back and forth, peering at stones, looking for the little name that was part of our extended family. I was about to give up when Andy called from a distance, "Here it is!" We brushed the newly cut grass off the stone and placed a flower on it. I swallowed hard, remembering the tears and the unanswered questions. We were quiet for a moment and then talked about life, about how fragile it is and how often we take it for granted. We walked slowly back to the car, and Andy commented on how Aunt Char and Uncle Bob went on with life, pastoring, raising their other two daughters, and going on to do missions work.

"Yes, it was hard, but they didn't get bitter," I replied. "They only became more committed, more compassionate. It reminds me of that quote, 'Only one life, 'twill soon be past; only what's done for Christ will last.'"

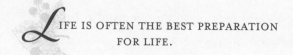

LIFE IS OFTEN THE BEST PREPARATION FOR LIFE.

Later, as I waved to my son, with his engaging, crooked grin, I suddenly thought how wonderful he was and how grateful I was for him—for his life. How good—and how rare—it was to spend a sunny afternoon with him. I drove to the retreat center to prepare for the evening session, aware that somehow I was prepared to speak after all.

I have found that *life* is the best preparation for life. Yes, we need thoughtful planning. Prayerful preparation and a disciplined study of God's Word are essential, because we cannot give out of what we do not have. But, just like my physical, day-to-day life, my spiritual life also has interruptions, "detours" onto the side roads of life where God teaches me so eloquently, whether by a shattering tragedy or a minor inconvenience. I used to believe that in order to speak and to write books I needed knowledge from other places. While I gain much

from reading and from listening to others, I've
learned that the most authentic material I have is
me and the message that God is writing in my
at-times-messy, unpredictable life.

Although I had less time to study for the retreat, I
realized that spending that afternoon with Andy was
maybe the most important part of my day—my week,
for that matter. After all, what was I going to speak
about? The gift of life. And it is in the crucible of
ordinary life, when we welcome His presence, that
He speaks to us and reminds us about what is important. We often make the Christian life more complicated that it needs to be. It is simple, really, to have
an awareness of God, even in the most mundane of
days, as we see in these words, penned by an
unknown writer:

> To be with God wondering, that is adoration
> To be with God gratefully, that is thanksgiving
> To be with God ashamed, that is confession
> To be with God with others on your heart, that is intercession.

How can we really follow Jesus these days? We can
study His example: He simply "went about doing
good" (Acts 10:38) and frequently took time to be

alone and pray. Our normal, everyday life is not something to just "put up with" until we get to heaven. It is true that distractions can cause us to temporarily detour from our normal path, and it's important to have healthy boundaries. But God truly is in everything, and we can learn to watch for His presence even when we find ourselves on a side road.

Lord, forgive me for attempting to orchestrate Your message when what You want to do is write Your message on my life. You have said that Your strength is made perfect in weakness. I am willing, Lord. I humbly place my weak, powerless, and ordinary life into Your hands. Give my hands strength to do physical tasks, my heart courage to do right, and my mind and heart wisdom to discern You in all of life. In Jesus' name I ask this, amen.

A man's heart plans his way, but the Lord directs his steps.

PROVERBS 16:9

HOLINESS IS NOT A STATE TO BE GAINED BY GOING AWAY FROM
LIFE, BUT BY ENTERING INTO IT IN THE MOST VITAL WAY.

Grace Brame, quoted in *The Ways of the Spirit* by Evelyn Underhill

CHAPTER THIRTY

The Gift of Peace

*L*ast Christmas I wandered the shopping center, looking at sweaters, books, games. As I shopped (and exchanged some things I'd already bought in my quest for the "perfect" gift), it occurred to me that the gifts I really longed for my family to have were not things I could wrap and put under the tree. If they were, I would give confidence to one child, self-discipline to another, involvement in a good church to yet another. Certainly I could encourage or make suggestions. But the fact is, it was up to each person to work toward these things.

As I hurried to get through my shopping list, out

of nowhere came a question: *What's the real gift that you need?* It almost seemed as if God were asking me what I wanted for Christmas! As I thought about it, I realized, *I need peace!* I need the deep, settled peace that only God can give. Maybe I need it so much right now because I am having to redefine the word *family* as my children need me less. And because I'm buying far too many sympathy cards these days, for friends our own age who are losing their spouses as well as their parents.

I also need peace because, I confess, I tend to worry. This is truly where I most need to grow in God, to let go of worries and rest in His peace. And I can be creative in the way I worry—what I worry about depends on the day. Those who don't know me well don't realize that beneath my calm exterior often lies a raging torrent of anxiety and worry that threatens to overwhelm me. And for some quirky reason—maybe because of my role as a mother—I think I have to make sure everything comes out right for those I love the most. I know that is neither logical nor possible, but knowing something in your head and believing it in your heart can be two different things.

Two weeks before I started my Christmas shopping last year, Bill gave me a wonderful, surprising gift. He told me to set aside four days between the holidays, in which he and I would celebrate my turning fifty. He said it would be a surprise. Was it ever!

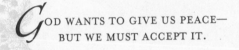

GOD WANTS TO GIVE US PEACE—
BUT WE MUST ACCEPT IT.

When I was a little girl, my parents liked to take our family to our cabin on the other side of Glacier Park in late fall, after the summer work was done. One year we encountered an early blizzard on the way, and the highway was closed. We were near an old lodge called the Izaak Walton Inn, on the edge of Glacier Park, so my father did the unthinkable: He splurged and booked two rooms for all of us—my parents, my grandmother, and five of us children. We children were ecstatic because we rarely got to stay in a hotel. Spending time with my family in this special place, with its high ceilings, massive stone fireplace, and cozy dining room, while the storm raged outside was a moment in time—a special memory.

I had heard that the inn had been restored and casually mentioned to Bill that someday I'd like to take him there. Bill decided my fiftieth birthday would be the "someday," and since the train stopped in front of the inn (if there were any passengers), he spent six months planning a surprise train trip home to Montana. By the time we got to the train station in Portland, I had an inkling that we were going to the Izaak Walton Inn, but seeing my extended family and some lifetime friends show up at the train station to go along was a shock. It was like a traveling "This Is Your Life." It took several hours for me to lose the stunned look on my face.

Of course I accepted that gift. I just got on the train, not knowing for sure what was happening, and enjoyed the journey immensely. I had done none of the work, none of the planning and organizing; Bill had done it all.

Almost a full year has passed since I told God how much I needed His peace. Accepting His peace reminds me of that surprise train ride home, a time of sheer, unexpected pleasure. Because I knew and trusted Bill, I just got on the train. And because I know and trust God, I believe He wants to give us the best gifts—to surprise us with joy and to shelter us from the inevitable storms of this life by giving us His peace.

Jesus said, "My peace I give to you; not as the

world gives do I give to you. Let not your heart be troubled, neither let it be afraid" (John 14:27). A friend who has a serious brain tumor told me yesterday, "I don't understand it, but I have a deep, unshakable peace." My worries pale beside what my friend is facing. I only know that God has given His peace and somehow my friend has accepted it.

What a great gift exchange! We give God our worries; He gives us His peace! We can get "on the train" of His grace with everything that we are, everything we have, and be at peace, knowing He has done all the work. He is our perfect peace offering, and by His death, He has "won" peace for us. It is for me to gratefully receive it as I yield to Him all that I hold dear.

Do you have real peace? Peace is not absence of conflict at any cost; it is the quiet assurance that you are in the right place, the right situation, and it comes from trusting God in that situation. It does not mean that everything is wonderful. But we receive His peace when our will is aligned with His and we know that He is in control, regardless of our circumstances.

Lord, how profound and sweet is Your peace—and how often we simply do not accept it. Instead, we continue to strive and to struggle in our own "strength." Forgive us, Lord. Thank You for patiently waiting until we yield our all to You. Remind us that it is only when we rest in You, God, that we know true, settled peace deep in our souls. We praise You, Lord, for Your perfect peace. In Jesus' name, amen.

Don't worry about anything; instead, pray about everything. Tell God what you need, and thank him for all he has done. If you do this, you will experience God's peace, which is far more wonderful than the human mind can understand. His peace will guard your hearts and minds as you live in Christ Jesus.

PHILIPPIANS 4:6-7, NLT

In the dark days of the Reformation in Europe,
Luther wrote to a friend: "I am against those
worrying cares which are taking the heart out of you.
Why make God a liar in not believing his wonderful
promises, when he commands us to be of good cheer,
and cast all our care upon him, for he will sustain us?
Do you think he throws such words to the winds?
What more can the devil do than slay us?
Christ has died for sin once for all, but for
righteousness he will not die but live and reign.
Why then worry, seeing he is at the helm?
He who has been our Father will also be the
Father of our children."

Alfred E. Cooke, *Treasury of the Christian Faith*

CHAPTER THIRTY-ONE

Seeing His Face

There were twenty of us in the waiting room that Sunday, going back and forth to the birthing room where our son and daughter-in-law were. I'd never been this close to birth when I wasn't the one in the bed. It hadn't seemed that long since Bill and I were in a labor room waiting for Jon's birth. Now he and Brittni were about to become parents. I was nervous and excited at the same time, remembering the pain and uncertainty of birth. And, of course, Brittni's mother was excited, sharing a special empathy with her daughter. For several months now, I'd had a sonogram of this baby tucked in my Bible at Psalm

139. As I studied the shadowy picture, I would privately wonder about him and pray over him. I was convinced even then there was a strong resemblance to Jon.

This baby—our first grandchild—was getting a grand reception. All of Brittni's family and all of Jon's family were there to welcome this long-anticipated child into the world. It was a party, of sorts. As the hours dragged on, we ordered pizza and ventured guesses as to what time Will Estep Carmichael would actually arrive. Finally, as we stood outside the door at 10:35 that evening, we heard a baby's cry. He was here! Finally we could see him, hold him, touch him.

Later we stood around and exclaimed over Will: "Look, he has Grandpa Carmichael's lip." "He has the Estep eyes." As Brittni snuggled him, she could see her own father's distinctive hairline. As Bill and I held him for the first time and looked with wonder into his little face, I thought, *It's Jon all over again.* Still, he is uniquely and wonderfully himself.

Later still, as we drove back to our motel, Amy was quiet.

"What do you think, Ames?" I asked her. My beautiful sixteen-year-old daughter leaned her head on the seat ahead of her. "I don't look like anybody in this family," she said.

Here was another reminder that a woman somewhere in Korea had given birth to a child she was unable to keep. Her loss was our gain, but it's also a loss for Amy not to know who she looks like. "Amy, you're grafted in," I tried to explain to her. "It's sort of like becoming God's child. We're all adopted into God's family, and over time, we hope we start to look like Him. Sure, your heritage is Korean, but you're pretty much a Carmichael."

Amy's comment made me think. As painful as it is for Amy not to know her birth family, God has used this loss to add depth and richness to our family. We've been privileged to experience not only the miracle of birth but the miracle of adoption as well. Birth is an amazing, all-consuming experience, where we partner with the Creator in a miracle. But adoption is a miracle too—the not knowing, the waiting. It is a thrilling moment, in both birth and adoption, to finally *see* that long-awaited one's face. The bonding time for adoption—especially if the child is older—takes some time and special attention. When Amy first arrived at age three, I wasn't sure how to connect with her. God seemed to be urging me, "Nourish her with your eyes." I tried to give Amy lots of smiling, warm eye contact, looks of approval and acceptance, and they did seem to help.

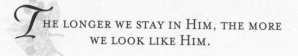

*T*HE LONGER WE STAY IN HIM, THE MORE WE LOOK LIKE HIM.

After Will was born, he lay quietly, his eyes wide open. As we gazed back at him, it seemed we could see forever in his dark blue eyes. We covered him with kisses. "Who are you, most wonderful child? We are so glad you are here. We love you so much!" Whenever I am with Will, I never tire of looking at him, of memorizing every detail. The reality of Will is so much better than the joyful anticipation of his arrival.

Sometimes when I think about Jesus, He seems like a "sonogram" to me. I study His "picture" in the Word, ponder His truths, and trust Him by faith. I know He's there and that His faithful promises and grace hold me, but, as the Bible says, it can be like seeing through a glass darkly. I long for the time when I can actually *see* Him face-to-face. I wonder what it will be like to be in His physical presence after a lifetime of expectation. Surely the anticipation—as great as it is now—will pale in comparison.

As a grafted-in heir, I hope my resemblance to Him is growing. I know it takes time. Will's birth reminds me that the miracle isn't complete yet. But we read in 1 John 3:2: "We can't even imagine what we will be like when Christ returns. But we do know that when he comes we will be like him, for we will see him as he really is" (NLT). Someday our eyes will really see him. On that day our "family resemblance" to our Father will be complete.

Ask yourself these three questions:

1. *Am I truly His?* To become His children we must be born again, and that is a holy mystery. Read John chapter 3 and Romans chapter 5. Also Romans 10:8-10 and Psalm 51.
2. *Is my resemblance to Him growing?* It takes study and time to know God's real character, His true nature. God has chosen to reveal His character to us in the pages of His Word and through the person of His precious Son, Jesus. The more you feed on God's truth, the clearer will be your picture of the one who loved us enough to die for us.

3. *Do I long for His return?* We long to be with those we love. "There is in store for me the crown of righteousness, which the Lord, the righteous Judge, will award to me on that day—and not only to me, but also to all who have longed for his appearing" (2 Timothy 4:8, NIV).

 Lord, how good it is to belong to You—even though it is a walk of faith and sometimes we don't see so clearly. I pray, Lord, that we will spend so much time with You in Your Word and in prayer that we will grow to look more and more like You. May we see the world through Your eyes and live for the day when we will actually see You face-to-face. In Jesus' name, amen.

Behold, the tabernacle of God is with men, and He will dwell with
them, and they shall be His people. God Himself will be with them
and be their God. And God will wipe away every tear from their
eyes; there shall be no more death, nor sorrow, nor crying. There
shall be no more pain, for the former things have passed away.

REVELATION 21:3-4

WE SHALL SEE HIS LOVELY FACE
SOME BRIGHT, GOLDEN MORNING,
WHEN THE CLOUDS HAVE RIFTED,
AND THE SHADES HAVE FLOWN;
SORROW WILL BE TURNED TO JOY,
HEARTACHES GONE FOREVER;
NO MORE NIGHT, ONLY LIGHT,
WHEN WE SEE HIS FACE.

Norman J. Clayton, taken from an old hymnbook

About the Author

Along with her husband, Bill, Nancie Carmichael has been involved in publishing since 1979, when they founded Good Family Magazines, which include *Christian Parenting Today; Parents of Teenagers;* and *Virtue.* Although the magazines are now owned by Christianity Today, Inc., Nancie remains editor-at-large of *Virtue* and still writes The Deeper Life column for that magazine. She leads Bible studies and is also a speaker at seminars and conferences and at women's retreats throughout the United States and Canada.

Nancie has written several books with her husband, including *Lord, Bless My Child; Lord, Bless This Marriage; The Best Things Ever Said about Parenting;* and *601 Quotes about Marriage & Family* (all published by Tyndale House); and *That Man: Understanding the Difference* (Thomas Nelson). Nancie has also written *Your Life, God's Home* (Crossway) and *In God's Word* (Harvest House).

The Carmichaels have five children and are enjoying being first-time grandparents to one-year-old Will. They live in Sisters, Oregon.

Appendix

A listing of the issue of *Virtue* magazine in which each of the devotionals originally appeared.

1. A Call to Come Away—September/October 1990
2. Seeking a Grateful Heart—November/December 1990
3. The Everlasting Arms of Grace—January/February 1991
4. Open Hands, Trusting Heart—March/April 1991
5. Living Life's Parentheses—May/June 1991
6. Dismantling My Tents—September/October 1991
7. Singing in the Dark—January/February 1992
8. The Place Where God Speaks—July/August 1992
9. Leaving Home, Going Home—September/October 1992
10. On the Ragged Edge—January/February 1993
11. Ribbons of Joy (originally titled "Transitions Tied Up with Red")—November/December 1992
12. Leaving the Wilderness—July/August 1993